by Bruce Eaton

SIMON AND SCHUSTER
NEW YORK

NO EXPERIENCE NECESSARY

MAKE $100,000 A YEAR
AS A STOCKBROKER

Published by Simon & Schuster
A Division of Simon & Schuster, Inc.
Simon & Schuster Building
Rockefeller Center
1230 Avenue of the Americas
New York, New York 10020
SIMON AND SCHUSTER and colophon are registered trademarks
of Simon & Schuster, Inc.
Designed by Irving Perkins
Manufactured in the United States of America

10   9   8   7   6   5   4   3   2   1
Library of Congress Cataloging-in-Publication Data
Eaton, Bruce.
    No experience necessary.

    Includes index.
    1. Brokers.   2. Stock-exchange.   I. Title.
HG4621.E37   1987   332.6'2   86-14633
ISBN: 0-671-62290-0

For Linda. Thank you.

CONTENTS

INTRODUCTION

For some people, success is equated directly with dollars: the more money you make, the more successful you are. "Money's important to me—it's how society keeps score" is a familiar comment in the business world.

But obviously the amount of money on the scoreboard doesn't appear out of thin air. Money is given to us by other people in exchange for a product or service. Our success is nothing more than the sum total of our value to others. Unless we hold up our end of the bargain, the number on the scoreboard can plummet quickly.

This book is about making money, but it is also about building a strong foundation for a long career as a respected professional in your community. Success can be permanent if the right materials are used. I know, because I've seen them work for countless stockbrokers across the country.

During my years as a stockbroker, I not only learned the ins and outs of the profession firsthand, but also had the privilege of working with some of the top brokers in the business. Although they had come from all walks of life, the traits they had that made them successful were remarkably similar.

Since then, I've trained over four thousand stockbrokers in key aspects of their jobs. While following the careers of my former students, I've discovered that the successful ones also have the same characteristics that lead to achievement. This experience provided the basis for this book. It is a blueprint for success in a profession that places no limits on how fast you can climb the ladder or how far you can climb. (Although stockbrokers are given various titles by their respective firms—registered representative, account executive, financial consultant, financial planner—stockbroker or broker is the title most widely recognized by those outside the brokerage industry and is therefore used throughout this book.)

Curiously, many people outside the brokerage industry, and even some of those within it, are not aware of the excellent job done by thousands of stockbrokers in bringing Wall Street to Main Street. The media, for example, focus far more attention on money managers, arbitrageurs, and big-time business executives. Stockbrokers work out of the spotlight, surfacing in the public eye only when a member of the ranks goes astray. What's often overlooked is how well successful stockbrokers serve their customers. Fortunately, the lack of publicity surrounding the accomplishments of these brokers hasn't deterred them from continuing to push their performance standards even higher. It has, however, kept most people unaware of what being a stockbroker is really all about.

While stockbrokers come from every walk of life and usually have experience in other careers, most of the outstanding brokers are people who wouldn't trade their careers for any other in the world. Countless times I've heard some variation of the comment, "I never would have thought that I could be a stockbroker unless someone had talked to me about it." That "someone" is usually a friend or relative already in the business. It's not that the profession is a secret society open only to those with the right contacts, it's just that Wall Street has relied on word of mouth—an inefficient means at best—to spread the message of opportunity. The best messengers are those who've already cashed in that opportunity.

It's my sincere hope that this book will change that.

1

THE CHANCE TO HAVE IT ALL

What do the following people have in common?

> NAME: Ken Latham   AGE: 25
> PROFESSION: Industrial management
> STATE: Pennsylvania

> NAME: Valerie Freeman   AGE: 30
> PROFESSION: Public relations/advertising
> STATE: Florida

> NAME: Richard Desiderio   AGE: 48
> PROFESSION: Insurance sales
> STATE: California

> NAME: Bob Cranshaw   AGE: 21
> PROFESSION: College student
> STATE: Kentucky

13

The answer is that they all became stockbrokers and achieved a six-figure income within three years!

It's no secret that the best jobs don't show up in the want ads. Anyone who's ever wanted a better job or a new career can attest to the lack of attractive alternatives on the surface of the job market. No one ever raises a flag and shouts, "Here's a great opportunity. Come and get it!" Most often, the best jobs are found in the invisible job market, where openings aren't trumpeted by ads, employment agencies, or headhunters. Positions get filled by the people who do enough digging to find them. Of course, if you know what you're looking for, the digging is always easier.

Ken, Valerie, Richard, and Bob knew what they were looking for in a job. Their searches all ended in a profession that offered them everything they wanted and more. A profession that may have just what you've been looking for, too.

What does it offer? Do you want high income potential? The sky's the limit. How about independence? You're an entrepreneur, your own boss. Is it dynamic? You bet. You're right in the middle of what's going on in the world. What about "psychic income," or personal satisfaction? It offers that too. You're helping other people with one of the most important parts of their lives.

Does it take an advanced degree, years of learning the ropes, a pile of start-up money, or the right connections to get into a profession that offers these advantages? Ordinarily, the answer would be yes. But there's one very big exception—a profession where the door is open much wider than you think. Who are the members of this profession? Stockbrokers.

Quite simply, no other field has the combination of earning potential and accessibility that investment sales offers. Any motivated and intelligent adult has the potential to become a successful stockbroker. Yet countless qualified people remain unaware of the opportunity of a lifetime, which may be only an interview away.

Why do people have difficulty envisioning themselves as stockbrokers? Consider for a moment the typical images the word "stockbroker" conjures up. Men with names like L. Todd Worthington III sit in plush offices with degrees from Harvard or Yale hanging on the walls. They have long martini-fueled lunches at exclusive clubs and make early "gone for the day" exits from the office with golf bags in tow. "Sure thing" investment tips line the already overstuffed pockets of nose-in-the-sky clients. Now add the impressions we get from advertisements: a frantic broker with a phone pressed to each ear trying to fit the last piece into a million-dollar puzzle, or a pin-striped guru who occasionally deigns to impart his wisdom to mere mortals.

It's no wonder that people think, "That career is off limits to someone like me." But each year thousands find out otherwise. Consider the following.

I come from a very middle-class family. I was never exposed to wealth or even thought about it much when I was in school. I studied art and journalism. When I graduated I went to work for an advertising agency—doing artwork, writing ads, designing logos, things like that. I started at $600 a month. About the time I left to handle public relations for the city housing authority, the wife of the ad agency owner became a broker.

I was making $12,000 a year and had about $1,000 to my name. I had the idea that something related to oil would be a good investment—this was around 1978. I felt intimidated even walking through the door of a brokerage office. I never would have done it unless I'd known someone in the business.

The oil stock I finally picked out went up 20 percent in a month. Beginner's luck, but I started to think, "My God, this is wonderful. This is what I could do all day for a living."

By this time I was totally fascinated with the stock market. I had read a number of books my broker had recommended and spent a lot of my lunch hours at her office trying to learn more. I was also "creating" myself right out of a job with the city—I'd turned around the program I was in charge of, and there wasn't much left to do. Somebody told me I should become a broker. At first I said, "No way, I've never even taken a business class in my life." He said, "You might be surprised." I walked into the manager's office one day and walked out with a job.

Before I became a broker, sales had always had a negative connotation. But if you're motivating someone to do something that's good for them, that's positive. I have to be the best possible person I can be for my clients and give them the best possible advice. I'm selling myself, and I want people to have faith and trust in me.

My first year in the business I made about $30,000. By my fourth year I was making $150,000. If you're helping people and you're providing them and their families with a better living, you earn it.

VALERIE FREEMAN

Valerie's income is not one in a million. Investment sales is the second-highest-paying widely practiced profession in the United States. Only doctors make more money. On the average, stockbrokers earn more than lawyers, dentists, accountants, or corporate managers. In fact, their incomes can exceed those of the top executives of the companies whose stocks they buy and sell.

In 1983, the average experienced stockbroker—representing all brokers with at least twelve months in the business—took home over $82,000. In 1984, a year with less sympathetic financial markets than 1983, the average experienced broker made "only" $64,000. In 1985, brokers showed their tremendous earning power once again. Average income for brokers with over one year of experience exceeded $79,000. First year brokers didn't exactly suffer: they averaged over $35,000 in earnings for the year. Keep in mind that these are average figures. Six-figure incomes of $100,000 and up are common. Brokers at the top make over $1,000,000 a year!

I majored in education at a large university. Before I even graduated I got a job working at a scrap metal company. I knew nothing about it, but they liked my vim and vigor and figured

I'd give them a fresh approach. I became the youngest person ever in management in the company. In three years I got to wear a lot of hats and got a lot of experience—enough to want to work for myself.

If you had asked me in college if I could see myself as a stock-broker my answer would have been, "Definitely not." I felt it was something I just didn't have the potential to do. Then I read an article in the paper and thought, "That kind of sounds like me." I have a cousin in the business, and I asked him if he thought I could do it. He said, "Absolutely. You're articulate, honest, and you work hard. That's what it takes."

I bought some books to improve my knowledge and then decided to go for it. At the time my wife told me, "I just don't think that anyone can walk in and be a broker. I think you have to have the right kind of training. Are you sure you know what you're doing?"

In college I had made the baseball team as a walk-on, which I think had a lot to do with me getting the job. The manager who hired me liked the fact that I'd had enough gumption to walk up to someone and tell them, "I'm better than the people on the field" and then go out and prove it. It showed that I could set a goal and stick with it.

I work under my firm's umbrella, but I work for myself. I know why I'm here. It's in my personality that I'm competitive. I made over $80,000 my first full year in the business, but it's not just the money. I want to prove my worth. I want to be someone that people think can really do them a service. I try to help them design a personal financial blueprint and then try to get them there as safely and quickly as possible.

KEN LATHAM

It's often been said that the best way to make money is to work for yourself. This is easier said than done. Starting a business involves a tremendous amount of risk. Eight out of ten small businesses fail within ten years, usually leaving the owners saddled with debt and with limited options for the future. No wonder most people are willing to forgo the upside potential of running a business for the security of knowing that they'll be able to make their mortgage payments and put food on the table.

Consider, however, someone offering to pay the costs of setting you up in your own business and even giving you a modest salary to hold you over until you got your business going. That's a different story, isn't it? Welcome to the unique entrepreneurial world of stockbrokers.

Although stockbrokers work for brokerage firms, they are very much in business for themselves. They are responsible for making the decisions that are at the core of running a business; finding customers and keeping them satisfied. They decide how hard to work in building their businesses. Although someone else signs the paycheck, the amount on each check is determined by the effort and skills of the individual broker. The more business done, the more money made. All the brokerage firm asks is a percentage of the profits. What the broker gets in return is an unbelievable bargain.

Brokers are trained at their firm's expense, a cost that can run up to $40,000. There's no such thing as getting set up. All the facilities—office space, furniture, phone, supplies—are provided. Nor do brokers face the problem of hiring people to help them run their business. The support staff is already in place. Brokerage firms also employ teams of experts to assist brokers in finding good investments. Advertising too is taken care of by the firm, not the broker.

In short, stockbrokers are entrepreneurs, but they avoid the financial risks and many of the headaches that are usually part and parcel of running one's own show.

What good is owning a business, though, if you have to scuffle for every nickel and dime? How many times have you said, "Just what this town needs—another pizza parlor?" There may not be room for another pizza shop in your town, but there is room for another successful stockbroker, for the following reasons.

Stockbrokers work with money, helping people protect their dollars and get more. The appeal of making money has been around for quite a while; it's not going to go out of fashion in our lifetimes.

For a long time stockbrokers were limited to the use of two basic tools: stocks and bonds. In the last decade, that has changed. Although stocks and bonds are still the central focus of the brokerage community, stockbrokers today may offer as many as 150 different investments, including retirement plans, real estate partnerships, precious metals, and even insurance. Brokers are now able to address just about every financial need they come across. The entire industry is shifting from a sales approach ("This is what I want you to buy") to a marketing approach ("Tell me what you need").

You might think that, given the flexibility and resources that today's brokers enjoy, they must have all the people with money to invest sewed up. Wrong. Here's what the experts say:

- According to a study by the Federal Reserve Board, stockbrokers are the most widely used source of financial advice among families earning over $50,000 a year. Even so, only 25 percent of these high-income families obtain advice from a broker, and less than 50 percent obtain advice from any source. Families in the $50,000-and-up income group hold almost $300 billion in liquid assets.
- The consequences of not receiving proper financial advice can be costly. The same Federal Reserve Board study showed that only one in five families with incomes of between $100,000 and $280,000 own municipal ("tax-free") bonds, while two out of three have savings accounts. This means that people in high tax brackets are more than three times as likely to have money invested at inferior interest rates and to be paying taxes on the interest, instead of holding an investment that offers tax-free interest and higher interest rates.
- Interest in investing is on the rise. The number of Americans owning shares of stock or mutual funds doubled between 1975 and 1985, reaching a record 47 million, according to a survey conducted by the New York Stock Exchange. This number continues to grow.
- In recent years, 77 percent of new shareowners were between the ages of 21 and 44. Tomorrow's big investors are getting started today.
- The "baby boom" generation has grown up and is making

money. A senior executive at a major brokerage firm believes that there are over 10 million people between the ages of twenty-five and thirty-four living in households with incomes of greater than $35,000. As they grow older, they will have more and more money available to invest.

There's plenty of room in the pool.

I studied operations management—how to run things more effi-ciently—in college. What set me apart was that I earned my independence. I learned how to use my time and worked my way through school. That's how I found out I got along with other people and had the motivation to do more than everyone else.

When everyone was sitting back waiting for the recruiters to come around, I was traveling across the state knocking on doors applying for jobs. I had several offers, but at the last minute I asked my older brother (a broker) about the brokerage industry. If it hadn't been for him, I would never have realized what being a stockbroker is all about.

This job has the two aspects I want in a career—helping people and making money. I like getting out and meeting people and giving them what they need. When people keep coming back, it makes you feel good. There's a lot of gratification.

People ask me how I know about all these investments. I tell them, "It's my job to know." You've got to be 100 percent com-mitted to learning, but it's fun to learn. You're dealing with the whole world.

I went to my fifth high school reunion last year. Nobody was even making close to what I make ($75,000 at the time, over $100,000 now). But you can't just see the money, you've got to see the people.

BOB CRANSHAW

There is no question that a stockbroker's world revolves around making money for his customers and for himself. But if the only attraction of being a stockbroker was money, the road to success in the profession would be long and barren with few travelers. There's so much work involved, there must be other benefits along the way.

Every single broker interviewed for this book, all extremely successful, mentioned "working with people" or "helping people" as the most enjoyable aspect of his or her career. This is certainly no coincidence. To do an effective job, a broker has to stand in the customers' shoes and try to understand their needs and concerns.

Stockbrokers have the opportunity to help people with a very important aspect of their lives—their financial health. It's impossible to put a price on the feeling that comes from helping others. However, the value of the service a broker provides can be spelled out in dollars and cents.

Let's say that someone in the 30 percent tax bracket has $10,000 in a passbook savings account, earning 5 percent. Because Uncle Sam is taking half of every dollar, the rate of return on the savings account is only 3½ percent—about one notch higher than if the money were buried in the back yard.

At the recommendation of his broker, the person takes the $10,000 out of his savings account (he has to give back the toaster) and invests in a tax-free municipal bond with a 7 percent return. Now he pays no taxes on the income—he keeps every cent. From 3½ percent to 7 percent—with one simple move, the return on the money doubles!

Not only do stockbrokers work with people, they work with a lot of people. A successful stockbroker has hundreds of clients of all ages and from every imaginable background. The experience of meeting people from all walks of life, many of whom you would never meet otherwise, can be unforgettable. One of my favorite clients was an auto worker who had fled to the United States from Communist rule in Eastern Europe. While learning a new language and a different way of life, he became a savvy investor, spending hours looking for good stocks to invest in. He relished an economic opportunity available in this country that too many people ignore. I will remember him far longer than the money I earned from his account.

It's not just working with people that motivates brokers, it's also the subject matter they work with. Few pursuits are more dynamic and challenging than investing. A stockbroker has to have her fingers on the pulse of the entire world. Not many occupations afford the chance to learn about what's going on around us on so many different levels.

A broker studies economics while following interest rates, politics while watching the federal budget, technology when a new computer appears. Changes in investors' attitudes involve psychology, population shifts, demographics, highs and lows in the market, history.

The scenery is constantly changing. No two days are the same. Yet within this constantly changing environment, a stockbroker has to make decision after decision and stand judged by the results. For those who enjoy a challenge, the thrill never wears off.

I grew up in the forties and fifties. Both of my parents were immigrants. College was out of the question—there just wasn't enough money. I've had a full-time job since I was fourteen, even in high school.

I worked for a tire company for eight years. Started off as a gas station attendant and moved up to territorial sales manager. I wanted to do something a little more rewarding, so I went into insurance in 1961. I tried my hand at management for a while, but decided I liked working with people one on one, so I went back into sales.

I really wanted to become a stockbroker because I wanted to offer a broader range of investments that could help me reach more people. My basic product is service. Everybody's got something to sell, but you're only as good as your service—attending to people's individual needs.

You get out of it what you put into it. If I'd stayed in insurance, I would have made $50,000 last year. It took me eight months to hit that level as a broker. It took me just another twelve months to double my income to $100,000.

RICHARD DESIDERIO

For many people, stockbrokers are surrounded by an aura of financial wizardry acquired from years of study at business school. How accurate is the image? Consider the following people: tennis pro, Navy pilot, computer salesman, dairy farmer, hospital administrator, high school principal, advertising sales manager, television programmer, FBI agent, cleaning fluid salesman, actor, minister, restaurant manager. Every one of them is now a successful broker.

Sure, there are some successful MBA's in the business. I also know of quite a few who didn't make the grade. Why? There's more to being a good broker than intelligence. As one brokerage executive explains, "If a person has a degree from a respectable college, he's smart enough to understand the business. Attitude and motivation are far more important. I don't look at what someone's done so much as how well they've done it."

What about the "males only need apply, prior sales experience preferred" sign that hung outside brokerage offices for many years? It's gone with the times. Not too many years ago, women stockbrokers were about as common as women in professional hockey. Today women account for approximately 25 percent of the new brokers hired by brokerage firms.

As for prior sales experience, whereas it was once considered a virtual necessity, brokerage firms are now finding that many, in some cases a majority, of their top brokers are coming from non-sales backgrounds. Having a background in sales doesn't hurt, however. It's a good way of showing that you can succeed in a competitive, entrepreneurial environment. The customer-centered approach required of today's broker is quite removed from the "this is what I have to sell, so this is what you're going to buy" philosophy commonly associated with sales, though.

By now you're probably wondering how someone with no financial background can give other people financial advice. As we'll discuss in a later chapter, all brokers are required to complete a sixteen-week training period before they can deal with the public. Everyone starts out more or less equal. Also, much of investing is based on common sense and experience, neither of which can be gained in a classroom. Your level of knowledge is determined by your commitment to learning.

There is practically no age that makes you too young or too old to become a stockbroker, either. Consider the four brokers you just met. Bob started right out of college. Richard began a second career at the age of forty-eight. For Ken and Valerie, becoming a stockbroker proved to be the right choice after beginning their professional careers in different directions.

Wherever you live, chances are good that one of the over seven thousand brokerage offices in the country is nearby. Now that you know the door is open, let's take a closer look at what goes on inside.

2

A DAY IN THE LIFE OF A STOCKBROKER

7:00 A.M. *Anne Mathews wheels her car into the office parking lot. The lot is virtually empty, as is the office inside. Only the head bookkeeper and Mike Briggs are there to greet Anne. (After twelve years in the business and over a million dollars a year in production, Mike doesn't show any signs of letting up. The only way to beat him into the office is to spend the night.)*

Anne grabs a cup of coffee and her copy of the Wall Street Journal *and heads off to her private office. She's only had a private office for a few weeks and the thrill still hasn't worn off—it sure beats sitting out in the board room. It's a symbol that Anne has arrived; she's not just another broker any more.*

After quickly flipping through the Journal, *Anne starts the day the same way she does every day: totalling up her business from the day before.*

Anne thumbs through the slips of paper that confirm each of the buy and sell orders she entered the day before, stopping to

*record a number from each slip on her calculator. The number is
the commission paid by each customer for each transaction. Like
anyone running a business, Anne wants to know where she stands
in exact dollars and cents.*

*The total comes to $1,843. Not bad, Anne thinks, but not good
enough. Her goal is a $40,000 month, and she needs to average
$2,000 a day to hit it. Anne wants her own secretary (commonly
referred to as a sales assistant)—right now she shares one with
another broker—to go along with her new office. The best way to
get one is to put even bigger numbers on the board and let the
numbers do the talking.*

*Anne writes the total down in the book she uses to chart her
progress day by day, week by week, and month by month. Last
month she did over $23,000 in production, a long way from the
$2,300 she totaled for her first month in business a mere thirty
months ago.*

Stockbrokers work on a commission basis. For each buy or sell
order the customer is charged a commission fee. The fee is determined by the type of investment and the amount of money
involved. The percentage can vary greatly. For example, a $10,000
investment in a mutual fund might cost the customer 8 percent
or $800, while the same amount of money invested in a stock
selling for $20 a share would cost around 2 percent or $200. For
most stock and bond orders the commission is less than 3 percent
of the amount invested.

Brokers receive a percentage of each commission fee. The
remainder is kept by their firms. The percentage received by the
broker varies from firm to firm and investment to investment but
typically falls in the 30-to-45 percent range. The industry-wide
average is 38 percent. Generally, the more commissions a broker
generates, the greater the percentage that goes to the broker.

The amount of gross commissions a broker generates is commonly referred to as *production*. Successful brokers are often
called "big producers" or "big hitters." The elite of the profession
are the million-dollar producers—brokers who produce over $1
million in commissions in a single year. That's an annual income
of over $400,000! To earn $100,000 in a single year takes over

$250,000 in production, a total well within reach of a hard-working broker like Anne.

Brokers are usually paid by the month. The amount is based on their total production. As a result, brokers think of their business in terms of months. They'll say, "What kind of a month are you having?" or in Anne's case, "I'm shooting for a big month." The months add up to the most important number to every broker: the "year" or annual production total.

A broker's annual production does more than determine his annual income. It is a numerical tag that determines his place in the pecking order, not only in his office but in his firm. Even with the increasing emphasis in the brokerage industry on meeting the needs of the customer, the production dollar still has the final say. Brokerage office managers are recruited from the ranks of top producers. A manager's attention turns toward the bigger producers in the office—after all, they pay the freight. The bigger the production total, the more "perks" a broker receives. In a profession that offers a high degree of personal freedom, success brings even more independence.

7:30 A.M. *Anne reaches into her briefcase and pulls out a legal pad with her agenda for the day, which she prepared the night before. On the first page is a list of fifty names and phone numbers. The people on the list have two things in common. They're local business owners, and Anne has never spoken to any of them before. They are prospective customers or prospects. She wants to reach them early in the morning before they get too busy to talk. Anne picks up her phone and dials the first number. "Hello, Mr. Richards? This is Anne Mathews from the investment firm of Huxley Buckley. How are you today?"*

Anne is looking for more than pleasant conversation. She is looking for new customers. She immediately gets down to business. "I'm calling to offer my services in helping you put your money to work. Are you currently investing?" Anne wants to find out if Mr. Richards is in a position to take advantage of her services and if he has an interest in doing so.

Anne talks with Mr. Richards for almost ten minutes. The conversation culminates in Anne setting up an appointment later in the week to discuss Mr. Richards' situation in further depth. Most of Anne's calls aren't as successful. By 9:00 she has called all fifty numbers, talked to twenty-two people, and had only two more people show enough interest to warrant a follow-up.

As Anne glances at her watch she remembers her first months in business, when she prospected all day—it was the only thing she had to do. Anne has other prospects to call in the afternoon, but it's time for her to focus her attention on another list of people, that of her existing customers.

The majority of a broker's customers share two characteristics. They didn't know their broker prior to their business relationship, and it was the broker who initiated the relationship.

Customers are the lifeblood of any business. After a broker hangs up his shingle, however, he can't just sit back and wait for the customers to stream in the door—they won't. Brokers have to seek out their clientele.

The search for customers is called *prospecting*. Brokers contact prospective customers or *prospects* in a number of ways: in person, through the mail, or, most commonly, by telephone. The broker will try to learn enough about the prospect to be able to make a suitable investment recommendation. Providing advice isn't enough, though. Only if the prospect makes an investment through the broker does the broker earn a commission.

Turning a prospect into a customer is a delicate process and is relatively difficult to complete. It can take less than a week or many months. Not only must the prospect be willing and able to invest, the broker has to be able to motivate the prospect to act through a combination of professional ability and personal rapport. Only a small portion of a broker's prospecting efforts bear fruit. As a result, brokers must spend a major part of their time prospecting in order to build and sustain a successful business.

9:00 A.M. For the past week, Anne has been studying Willco Corp., a stock recently recommended by her firm's research department. Anne likes to be thoroughly familiar with an investment before she recommends it to her customers. The extra digging not only helps her find better investment opportunities, but it increases her confidence in her recommendations. This is no small matter when you're asking someone to invest thousands of dollars.

Anne has decided that Willco's stock is a good buy. It appears to be worth much more than its current price. Today she is going to recommend an immediate purchase of Willco Corp. to fourteen of her customers, for whom such an investment would be appropriate.

"Hello, Mr. Herbick? This is Anne Mathews. I have an idea I think we should take action on today. The company is Willco Corp...."

Over the next hour and a half, Anne reaches eleven of the customers on her list and receives orders from nine of them. The commissions total over $2,400—about $900 of which will show up in Anne's next paycheck. It may seem like a lot of money for not much work, but consider the untold hours Anne spent finding and developing the customers, not to mention the time she spends selecting the right investments for her customers.

Stockbrokers are often referred to as "financial physicians." They diagnose people's financial problems and then prescribe appropriate solutions. In this case, Anne is recommending Willco Corp. to her clients who need a growth investment.

Brokers must follow the rule of "know your customer." Any investment they recommend must be appropriate for a customer. What's good for a retiree might not be as good for a young executive. The "know your customer" rule not only helps investors, it also helps brokers. The more a broker knows about a customer, the easier it is to find investments that fit the customer's exact needs.

Once a broker has identified a person's need and even gone as far as deciding what type of investment will meet that need, however, the job has just begun. Anne determined that some of her customers needed a growth-oriented investment, but she was faced with thousands of choices. Some will prove to be profitable—as she believes Willco will—but others will turn out to be lemons.

The responsibility of selecting investments rests squarely in the hands of each individual broker. Although brokers receive considerable guidance from their firm's research departments in selecting investments, they make their own decisions on what to recommend to their customers.

The process of matching people's financial needs to good investments is the essence of a stockbroker's craft.

10:30 A.M. *Anne entered each order for Willco immediately after the customer gave the go-ahead. By the time her last presentation is winding up, the office wire operator has already received word that the first orders have been filled. As Anne pauses for a minute to check on the morning's activity in the stock market, the phone rings. One of her customers, the usually affable Mr. Backman, is on the warpath. "What's going on with you people! I've been waiting over a week for that dividend check I was supposed to get..."*

Brokers are just the first link in the chain of an investment transaction. The actual trading of securities is conducted at the various exchanges set up for this purpose. The New York Stock Exchange receives the most attention, but there are a number of others. Typically, a broker relays an order to a wire operator in the office, who sends it over a sophisticated communications system to the appropriate exchange. Brokers follow the activity on the exchanges with machines that provide up-to-the-minute price quotes. No matter where they work, they are only seconds from the action.

No matter what the investment, one result is always the same: paperwork. Fortunately for brokers, most of the paperwork is handled by the office operations department. This is where bills are sent out, payments are received, checks are mailed, and customers' monthly statements are prepared.

However, brokers still have the responsibility of making sure that the operations side of their business runs smoothly. The instructions of their customers, whether it be to buy 1,000 shares of Mobil Oil or mail out a check for $100, must be relayed to the operations staff accurately and promptly.

It's only natural when a firm handles thousands of transactions for thousands of customers involving millions of dollars that errors will be made. Regardless of where the fault lies, in the eyes of the customer the broker and the firm are one and the same. A broker has to make sure that any problem is cleared up quickly or risk losing the customer.

11:00 A.M. *With Mr. Backman's errant check now located and on its way, Anne continues checking on the activity in the stock market. As she punches up price quotes for the stocks her customers own, something catches her attention. Carter Technology is down a point. Anne recommended the stock at 21 six months ago. It is now trading at 17½. Carter's performance has been less than satisfactory, especially in light of the fact that overall the stock market has been rising. She realizes that it's time to make a decision. She quickly checks the news page on her quote machine for any late-breaking news on Carter. There is none. She calls the analyst at headquarters who follows the stock. He knows of no reason for the sudden drop. Anne still knows only one thing: she has customers who are losing money. She remembers a time a year ago when she was faced with a similar situation. That time she held the stock. It kept dropping, and her customers ended up with sizable losses.*

Anne decides that it's better to protect her customers from any further losses than hope for a turnaround. She looks up the customers who own Carter Technology, and within ten minutes of the price drop she has begun calling them to recommend selling the stock.

12:00 noon. *Anne finishes her last call and sells the last shares of Carter Technology. It's never easy taking a loss, but it's part of the business. Anne knows that no matter how many good investments she recommends—and she has an excellent track record—one big loss can reflect badly. Most people were thankful for the guidance. Only one customer wanted to hold on to Carter, but Anne held firm in her recommendation and in the end the customer agreed.*

Several other brokers stop by Anne's office on their way to have a quick bite across the street. After four and a half hours of working nonstop, Anne decides she needs a break and reaches for her coat.

Brokers don't always have the luxury of taking time to make decisions. Changes in the financial markets sometimes allow only minutes for determining whether an investment should be bought, sold, or held. Even if decisions are made based on the best information available, no broker has a crystal ball. A broker has to accept the inevitability of being wrong sometimes.

12:45 P.M. Anne returns from lunch recharged. She enjoys shop talk, from the serious exchange of ideas to the endless ribbing that goes on among the brokers in her office.

Anne flips through the phone messages she received while she was out to lunch. Among them are a request for a research report and a question about a monthly statement. Anne will have her sales assistant handle these, along with calling back the customers who purchased Willco to let them know the exact purchase price.

One message requires an immediate return call. Mr. Sandusky wants to place an order for some Union City municipal bonds he's picked out. Anne takes Mr. Sandusky's order, thanks him for his business, and suggests that they get together in the near future. Mr. Sandusky makes his own decisions, but Anne still wants to learn more about his situation. The better the service she provides, the smaller the chance of a competitor wooing Mr. Sandusky away.

There's more to a broker's work than making investment recommendations. The companion of sales is service. Brokers provide customers with information on investing and, in cases like Mr. Sandusky's, handle orders for customers who choose to make their own decisions. Service requires attention to detail—somebody who makes a sizable investment doesn't want to wait until the bill comes in the mail to find out the exact purchase price. A broker's sales assistant is in many ways a one-person service department, taking care of customer requests and inquiries that don't require the broker's involvement.

Good service builds loyal customers. Poor service makes it very tempting for a customer to transfer her account to another brokerage firm, especially if a broker at the rival firm is prospecting her.

1:00 P.M. *Anne settles in for the afternoon, armed with a cup of coffee and her plan of action. On her desk she places a list of prospects. These prospecting calls will be different from the "cold calls" she made this morning. Anne has talked to everyone on the list at least once and some three or four times. Today she is going to try to turn these prospects into customers.*

In prior conversations, each of these prospects has complained about paying too much in taxes. Anne believes that an investment in tax-free bonds that her firm will be offering next week is an ideal opportunity for them all to cut their tax bills.

"Hello, Dr. Rutherford. This is Anne Mathews from Huxley Buckley Securities. Last time we talked you indicated that you wanted to cut your tax bill and earn a better return on your money. I think I have just the investment for you ..."

The success ratio of the number of orders Anne receives to the number of her presentations is far lower than that of this morning's calls. Three out of the seven people she talks to place orders. The investment turns out to be inappropriate for two of the prospects. Anne will get back to them with an investment that better fits their needs. The others are just plain noncommittal. They won't take action and won't give any good reasons why they won't.

Nonetheless, Anne has plenty to be happy about. The three prospects who have agreed to make an investment are no longer prospects. They've opened accounts and have joined her growing number of customers. The first order is not only the most difficult to get, but it also involves the most paperwork. For each new customer, Anne has to fill out a lengthy questionnaire.

One of the critical parts of a broker's job is opening new accounts—turning prospects into customers. That change takes place the moment a prospect makes an investment through a broker.

Although a new customer may be required to make a deposit before placing an order, usually an investor has a week to pay for an investment. This involves a tremendous amount of trust on the part of brokerage firms. Where else can you spend thousands of dollars using your word as your credit card? Before extending credit, however, brokerage firms review the background and credit rating of each customer. A detailed form, similar to a bank loan application, must be completed by the broker and approved by an officer of the firm before any transaction can take place.

3:00 P.M. While Anne is completing a new account form, Ben Haller, the office manager, pokes his head in her door. "Hey, leave some of those new accounts for the rest of the office," he jokes. Anne leads the office in opening new accounts—a major reason for her success—and Ben wants to let her know she's doing a great job. He's also dropped by to give Anne her bonus check for last month's production. "The only thing that would make me happier is giving you a bigger check for this month," he says.

As the office manager, Ben wears many hats: motivator, cheerleader, administrator, psychologist, police officer, and ombudsman. Although he's the boss, he's also a former broker and is sensitive to the demands and pressures his people face. Ben is the glue that holds the office together.

No person has more of an impact on a broker's working environment than the local office manager. It takes the right combination of people, leadership, and teamwork to create an atmosphere where a broker can flourish. The manager coordinates everyone's efforts to try to create a successful office. Brokers may be the stars, but they also rely heavily on a supporting cast. In addition, even though brokers are entrepreneurs, there's plenty of room for teamwork that will help everyone involved.

One important duty of an office manager is serving as a constable: that is, making sure that brokers comply with the rules and regulations of the industry. Unethical or improper actions can cost a firm a great deal in terms of reputation and dollars.

4:45 P.M. After almost two more hours on the phone with prospects and customers, Anne looks at her watch, packs her briefcase, and hurries out the door. She has a meeting with a customer at his nearby business.

5:00 P.M. *Anne's appointment is with Michael Rigby, owner of a commercial photography studio. Anne has met with Mr. Rigby once before, when she was prospecting him. This time Anne isn't interested in walking away with a sale. She just wants to get a more complete picture of Mr. Rigby's financial situation to find out where he needs help. Anne believes in a total financial planning approach. She believes that what's best for the customer is ultimately what's best for her.*

Anne and Mr. Rigby chat for almost an hour. Anne has prepared a list of questions as a guide, and she takes copious notes. She also tries to zero in on the thoughts and feelings behind Mr. Rigby's answers. Anne enjoys Mr. Rigby. He's a congenial fellow in an interesting field. She finds that meeting people like him is one of the highlights of her work.

Anne will analyze the information she's obtained over the next week, then come back to Mr. Rigby with her recommendations. Now, Anne has two more stops to make before she heads home for the day.

Not all of a broker's work is conducted inside the office. Brokers still make house calls.

To be effective, a broker has to earn people's trust and confidence. Brokers can't do their job unless customers provide them with detailed personal information and with money to invest. Given the highly sensitive nature of handling other people's money, it's no wonder that brokers spend a lot of time meeting with clients and prospects. In many ways, the most important sale a broker has to make is the sale of himself—his honesty, ability, and concern for the customer's best interests. The best way to make that personal sale is in person.

If it's not possible or convenient for a prospect or customer to come into a broker's office, the broker will arrange a meeting outside the office. Since it is important that a broker be in the office during market hours—the hours the stock exchange is open—it's only natural that most appointments are scheduled early in the morning or late in the day. Evening appointments are common. As one broker puts it, "If I had a dollar for every cup of instant coffee I've had while sitting at someone's kitchen table talking about investments, I could retire."

6:00 P.M. *After her appointment, Anne stops off at the health club she belongs to. She tries to exercise every day, playing a game of racquetball or taking a two-mile run on the jogging track. Exercise helps Anne stay fresh during her long hours behind the desk and helps her unwind from the constant pressure.*

After her workout, Anne stops to pick up a snack from a vending machine in the lobby. It will be a while before she eats dinner; she's heading back to her office.

When Anne arrives at the office, many brokers are still at their desks. Most of them are still in their first few years in the business. She rolls up her sleeves and reaches for the mountain of paper that has accumulated during the day in her "in" box.

The pile contains everything from newly issued research reports to procedure notices from the operations department, memos from her manager, and brochures from marketing. Most she throws out after a quick scan, but the rest go into her briefcase. Anne will read them over the weekend when she has more time.

7:00 P.M. *Anne spends the next hour in the same way she has spent most of her day: on the phone, calling customers and prospects. Most of these calls are to people she wasn't able to reach earlier. The rest are to customers who aren't readily available during the day—everyone doesn't work right next to a phone. Anne gets two more orders for Willco, which she'll enter in the morning, sets up an appointment with a customer, and uncovers two good prospects.*

8:00 P.M. *Enough calls for today. It's time to look ahead to tomorrow. Anne tears the list of today's calls off her pad, and on a fresh sheet of paper she starts to plan tomorrow's activities.*

8:30 P.M. *Ready to go home, Anne looks for her desk keys in her purse and finds the unopened envelope enclosing her bonus check.*

She opens it. She has a good idea what the amount is, but it's always satisfying to see exact numbers and your name next to them. The check is for $8,498.54. Adding the $2,136.47 in taxes that's been withheld, the total comes to $10,635.01 for a month's work. Anne figures her earnings for the first six months of the year. She has made $54,687.19. With the way her business is growing, she's certain to achieve her goal: to earn over $100,000 this year.

The rewards that are enjoyed by successful brokers like Anne are not a lucky windfall. They are the result of long hours. Building a successful business requires a major commitment of time and energy, especially in the first several years of a broker's career. Although there's no schedule posted on any bulletin board, a sixty-hour-plus work week is standard, including Saturdays and several nights a week. That doesn't include time spent out of the office reading research reports and keeping well informed.

Once a broker is well established the work hours shorten, but not too much. Successful brokers don't believe in the nine-to-five mentality. Like people at the top of every profession, they know that reward is based on effort.

Anne's income has climbed into the top 1 percent for all American adults. Let's take a look at what got her there.

Anne's energy and enthusiasm for her work are obviously a big factor in her success. Success in any endeavor is rarely achieved without plenty of old-fashioned hard work. Anne has put a lot of hours into achieving her goal.

Energy and enthusiasm aren't enough, though. They have to be channeled in the right directions. Anne has a clear understanding of what a successful stockbroker must do, and she knows how to go about doing it.

The first step in becoming a successful stockbroker is understanding that the objective of your business is no different from that of any other business, whether it's the corner newsstand or General Motors. The objective is profit. You are in business to make money for yourself and for your firm. If this sounds self-serving, keep in mind that your income is a by-product of your value to others.

Next, you must understand the fundamental principles of building a profitable business. These are:

1. Know the business. You must be knowledgeable about your field.
2. Develop a competitive product. You must turn your knowledge to creating a product that fills a need in the marketplace.
3. Market your product. You must go out and find customers.
4. Keep your customers. You must keep your customers satisfied and coming back.
5. Keep repeating the first four steps. To keep your business growing, you must stay ahead of the competition, keep attracting new customers, and keep your existing customers happy.

If you ask one thousand successful stockbrokers how they approach these five steps, you'll hear one thousand different stories. "My Way" is certainly the most popular song in the brokerage industry. But, even though every successful broker sings it a little differently, adding his or her own style and embellishment, the basic tune is the same.

Beyond the differences of personality and circumstances in each broker's formula for success, there lie the skills, principles, and attitudes that all successful stockbrokers have in common. These are the fundamentals of success, the "must do's" that successful brokers follow every day, often out of intuition.

In several years you could be in the same position as Anne, enjoying a view of life from the heights of success while preparing to climb even further. You don't have to trust to your intuition or luck to show you the way. The next six chapters will tell you what you have to do to get there.

3

LEARNING THE BUSINESS: FROM TRAINEE TO STOCKBROKER IN FOUR MONTHS

Often the biggest barrier to embarking on a new enterprise is knowing how to get started. For the would-be stockbroker, knowing where to begin chipping away at the mountain of material on investing might seem impossible. Fortunately, the first steps are clearly marked.

GETTING LICENSED: THE GENERAL SECURITIES EXAM

To protect the public against unfair or unethical practices in the brokerage industry, a number of supervisory organizations, including the Securities and Exchange Commission (SEC), the National Association of Securities Dealers (NASD), and the stock exchanges, act together as an industry police force. Not only do they monitor the ongoing activities of every broker, they also set the minimum standards for becoming a broker.

Of all the titles used to refer to full-service stockbrokers—

account executive, financial consultant, customers' broker, registered representative—none more accurately describes their role in the inner workings of Wall Street than *registered representative*. "Representative" implies that a broker is in effect the intermediary between customers and the employees of the firm who handle the actual buying and selling of securities. "Registered" indicates that before you can engage in any business with the public you must pass several licensing examinations and be registered with the New York Stock Exchange. The most important of these exams is the General Securities Exam, also referred to as the *GSE* or the *Series 7*.

The purpose of the General Securities Exam is to determine whether the broker-to-be has the threshold level of knowledge of the securities industry necessary for dealing with the public while working under reasonable supervision. The exam was developed by the New York Stock Exchange and is administered by the NASD. Passing the exam is an absolute requirement for becoming a stockbroker.

The requirements for taking the General Securities Exam for brokers seeking to be registered with the New York Stock Exchange are as follows:

1. You must be employed full-time for at least eight weeks by a member firm of the New York Stock Exchange. You cannot take the test without being sponsored by a brokerage firm. We'll discuss how to get hired in chapter 10.
2. You must be of legal age in the state in which you are employed.

The GSE is given on the third Saturday of each month in over thirty cities throughout the country. It consists of 250 multiple-choice questions. The exam is divided into two three-hour segments of 125 questions each. To pass the examination you must answer at least 70 percent correctly. Of the total number of people who take the exam each year, approximately 65 percent pass. However, the pass rate for broker trainees from many full-service firms is significantly higher.

The New York Stock Exchange will not grant you a license until you have been employed full-time for four months, regardless of when you pass the exam. Typically, a firm will allow a trainee two and a half to three months to study for the GSE and will use the rest of the time for additional training. This means that you can go from trainee to broker in sixteen weeks. For no other high-paying profession are the entry requirements this favorable.

In addition, almost half the states require you to pass a separate examination to be licensed in those states. This exam, however, consists of only fifty questions. Passing it poses no problem to anyone who can pass the GSE.

PASSING THE GSE

The sheer amount of material you must learn to pass the GSE makes studying for the exam equivalent to a semester in college in terms of the time, mental concentration, and energy required. Because the GSE tests your knowledge on a broad range of topics, studying for it will provide you with an excellent introduction to the field. Among the topics covered are:

- Investments, including stocks, bonds, options, retirement accounts, and mutual funds
- The regulations and procedures a stockbroker must follow
- Economic and security analysis
- How the securities markets operate
- How securities are taxed

In short, many areas that may be foreign to you at the moment will become completely familiar. While you're studying for the GSE, you'll be amazed at how much you can learn in a short period of time.

You needn't worry about deciding what to study for the exam. Your firm will either provide you with study materials or direct you to one of the several study courses that are offered by independent training companies. Most of your learning will be done in independent study. It will be up to you to cover the material at a sufficient pace. Your firm will probably supplement your studies with some type of review class before you take the exam. As with every challenge you will face as a broker, however, your success will be ultimately in your own hands.

THE DIFFERENCE BETWEEN GETTING LICENSED AND GETTING TRAINED

Getting licensed is like learning the alphabet, but there's a lot more to learning how to read. The GSE is an entrance exam, not a finishing exam. Becoming a broker is similar to becoming a lawyer. It's a long way from passing the bar exam to becoming the next F. Lee Bailey. Once you've learned the "what" of being a broker, you have to learn the "how."

The GSE is simply a piece of paper that tests your knowledge of basic concepts. It does not prepare you to work in a dynamic, interactive environment. There is simply no way that answering a multiple-choice question about a fictitious stock can prepare you for a real person saying to you, "I'm going to take early retirement next month. What should I do with my thousand shares of Ford Motor Company?" The GSE covers the legal guidelines for selling securities; it does not test your ability to make an effective sales presentation. It is intended to help protect your customers; it does not test your skills in prospecting. Although it tests your knowledge of investments, it does so only in a general, theoretical fashion. You will not be asked details about your favorite mutual fund and why you selected it, but a customer very well might do this.

All stockbrokers—from those at the top of the profession to the most mediocre—have passed the GSE. Where you end up on the ladder greatly depends on your ability to communicate with people and to apply your knowledge to the real world. Passing the exam merely allows you to go on to the next stage of learning: getting trained in the skills necessary to be successful.

BEYOND THE GSE: AN OVERVIEW OF TRAINING

Training programs vary from firm to firm and range from intensive to nonexistent. Fortunately, the "here's your desk and phone, good luck" attitude toward new brokers is fast becoming extinct. Every new broker represents an investment in time and money to the firm. Most brokerage firms believe that proper training is important to a broker's success and the firm's profitability. In fact, some brokerage firms estimate that they have as much as $40,000 invested in a new broker before the broker even makes that first prospecting call, most of it due to training expenses.

As a general rule, the larger the firm, the greater the likelihood that it will have a formal training program. At most national and major regional firms, this will be held at the firm's headquarters and may last several weeks. Although no two training programs are alike, their areas of emphasis are similar. They generally fall into three categories:

1. Marketing skills—how to prospect for clients and make effective sales presentations. Training in this area usually includes making practice prospecting calls and sales presentations in a setting that allows for constructive feedback from an instructor or fellow brokers.
2. Practical investment knowledge—actual investments and their applications. This segment will include lectures covering the details of specific investments offered by the firm, the type of investors they are appropriate for, and how investors can benefit from the investments.
3. Orientation—the "who, what, where, and how" of the firm. This covers everything from how to enter orders to where to get help answering a question.

Once you've passed the GSE and completed your training, you enter the best learning situation of all: real life.

WHERE MOST TRAINING TAKES PLACE: ON THE JOB

After a certain point, preparation is merely a form of procrastination. No matter how much you read, listen, or watch, the best way to learn anything is by doing.

All brokers will tell you that it seemed as though they learned more during their first week in business than in their entire training period. The first time your receptionist announces, "Mr. Johnson is here to see you," you'll feel like a parachutist who can't find his rip cord. With a little experience, though, meeting with a customer will seem no different from sitting down with a good friend.

Experience is the best teacher only if you show up in class, however. Don't be afraid to take on new challenges. Expect to make mistakes. Nobody ever does anything perfectly the first time around; those who try to wait until they're perfect usually end up doing nothing. Failure is merely the means by which we learn how we can improve. If you work to correct your mistakes, failure will lead you to fruition instead of frustration.

LEARNING FROM THE EXPERIENCE OF OTHERS

One of the other best ways to learn how to do something is to follow the example set by others. You can learn how to be successful by imitating success. Many a ball player has made it to the major leagues because he wanted to play "just like Willie Mays." The most successful broker in your firm still looks up to someone else.

There will certainly be an experienced broker in your office who really stands out as a professional, the person who makes you think "I want to be just like him" (or her). Adopt him as your role model. Look for the things that set him apart. If they can be copied, do it! You may not have the same personality as your model, but you can work just as hard and set the same high performance standards.

Don't be afraid to ask your model for advice. You're likely to discover exactly what one broker discovered: "The number one broker in my office really helped me get on track. I set up a weekly meeting with him to go over my prospecting and investment strategies. All that knowledge and experience—it's hard to believe the other brokers were just ignoring it."

Just as important as selecting a role model is avoiding the negative influences in your office. There will always be brokers who blame their performance on the market, the research department, the management, the weather, anything except themselves. Don't let these people drag you down with them. The only way to make it to the top is to look up. If co-workers don't share your goals, attitudes, and desires, avoid them when you're at the office.

TRAINING AND YOUR LOCAL OFFICE MANAGER

Regardless of the level of training offered by your firm, your local office manager will have the opportunity to take a very active role in the training of the new brokers in your office.

I know many managers who view launching their new brokers' careers as one of their most important functions. New brokers in these managers' offices are schooled and drilled daily in marketing skills and investment knowledge by the manager or by experienced brokers. On the other hand, there are managers who believe that training is superfluous. They take the "they can figure it out if they really want to" approach.

There's no question that a training-conscious manager can play an important role in the training of a broker. However, because the commitment can vary so much from manager to manager, this type of training is more an extra than something to be counted on.

THE MOST IMPORTANT PERSON IN YOUR TRAINING: YOU

Whatever training you receive, whether it's at a firm-wide seminar or a one-on-one meeting with your manager, is certain to be beneficial. Every bit of training helps. But true excellence can't be taught, it must be achieved. Your attitude and your desire to learn are far more important to your success than any help your firm, manager, or role model can give you. Training programs make critical information easier to obtain, but the absorption and use of this information is up to you. As a new member of the "$100,000-a-year club" at Paine Webber explained, "In this business, if you aren't willing to teach yourself, you aren't going to learn that much." Good training can eliminate a lot of trial and error when you're starting out. However, there are brokers who have become successful without any training at all.

In reality, your training period will never end until the day you retire. There's always something new to be learned that will help you do a better job for your clients or be more efficient in your work. Take advantage of every training opportunity that presents itself along the way. Remember, though, that every day presents an opportunity to learn something new if you are your own teacher.

THE RIGHT PERSPECTIVE

Finally, your perspective on the world around you will play a significant role in your success. The broader your perspective, the better a broker you'll be. You'll be working in an environment that extends far beyond your home and your office to every corner of the globe. The financial community won't revolve around you or even your firm. To really know what's going on, you have to look at the entire picture.

Be aware that you will never know everything, but don't let that stop you from trying. One of Merrill Lynch's most outstanding managers once told me, "I want my new brokers to know enough to have confidence in themselves and still be scared by what they don't know. The biggest danger is for a broker who learns a little to think he knows it all. It's relatively easy for a broker to know more than ninety-nine percent of the public. But he has to realize that there's an awful lot of territory in that last one percent." Take pride in what you know, but temper your confidence with humility. You must be able to accept being wrong. The easier it is for you to admit mistakes, the smaller the consequences of your mistakes will be.

Don't view other people using solely your personal financial goals and experiences. The average new broker is around thirty years old. The average age of the head of a family with a net worth of between $100,000 and $249,999 is fifty-six. What might be a small fortune to you could be pocket change to someone else. On the other hand, what's a small sum of money to you may represent someone else's life savings. The only way you can be of service to others is to put yourself in their shoes and leave your wants and woes at home.

PUTTING YOUR KNOWLEDGE IN ACTION

In chapter 1 you met four very successful brokers, Valerie Freeman, Ken Latham, Richard Desiderio, and Bob Cranshaw, each with an unquenchable thirst for knowledge concerning every aspect of their profession. If knowledge was the sole reason for success, however, we'd be wrapping up right here. What separates successful brokers from the pack is not only what they know, but also what they do—how they put their knowledge into action. In the pages ahead, we'll look closely at how successful brokers, including Valerie, Ken, Richard, and Bob, run their businesses.

4

THE ESSENTIAL PRODUCT OF
A SUCCESSFUL
STOCKBROKER

For years, stockbrokers were virtually guaranteed a leading role in every investor's investment planning.

Commission rates charged to customers were set by the Securities and Exchange Commission and were uniform throughout the industry. If an investor wanted to buy or sell securities, she had to go to a stockbroker and pay the established fee.

Investors relied on stockbrokers for another critical service: supplying information. Brokers were the primary conduit for research, opinion, and conjecture about Wall Street. Without an attentive broker, the average investor was operating in the dark.

The marketplace you'll be competing in as a broker is much tougher and more complex than even that of a decade ago. In 1975, commission rates were deregulated by the Securities and Exchange Commission. Brokerage firms became free to set their own rates. This event gave birth to discount brokerage houses. These firms offer an investor limited services—no research or advice—but charge significantly lower commissions than full-service firms do. Investors who make their own decisions now have an alternative available to paying full-service commissions and doing business with a full-service broker.

Also, the Information Age has reduced stockbrokers to just one of many sources of quality information available to today's investor. Coverage of the financial world is now on the front page of your paper. Television shows, radio programs, and magazines aimed at the individual investor abound. Personal computers make it possible for financial news and research to travel directly into a home or office without stopping at a broker's desk. Subscription advisory services bring some of the sharpest minds in the business no further away than the mailbox. With all these resources available, it's possible for an investor to be better informed than his broker.

Clearly, you cannot expect to be successful by being only an order taker or by swamping people with research. You'll have to offer investors something more for their money.

Does this mean that you'll have to be a pioneer in the Wall Street jungle to find success? Fortunately not. All you need do is follow the lead of the thousands of stockbrokers who have found where the opportunity lies in today's competitive environment.

FINDING THE GREATEST OPPORTUNITY

If you took a survey of American adults, asking, "Are you confident that your money is properly invested and your finances in perfect order?" how many "yes" answers would you get? Not many. I've posed the same question to groups all over the country and never had a positive response greater than 5 percent. The fact is that almost everyone has financial problems waiting to be solved. Richard Desiderio goes further. "Most people don't even know what their problems are. They know they have them, and that's about it. A big part of my job is to impress upon people that if they understand their problems, they can be solved."

What is it that holds people back from obtaining advice on financial matters? Most people like the idea of getting more for their money, and there are certainly plenty of opinions floating around at any given moment on how to make a buck. The point is that people aren't willing to accept just any advice on financial matters. They want the right kind of advice.

To begin to understand the type of advice people want, let's take a look at some other professions for a moment. Doctors, plumbers, engineers, and auto mechanics have one thing in common. They are problem solvers. Whether we have a pain in the chest or a knock in the engine, we approach problem solvers with the same expectations.

First, we expect *quality*. We expect that any advice we receive will be the result of professional judgment based on the best information available. Second, we expect the advice to be *personalized*. We want the solution to our problem, not someone else's. Third, we want the final *decision* to be made for us. If we knew what to do, we wouldn't have gone to the problem solver in the first place.

A problem solver who can meet these three expectations is of great value to us. We gladly give him our business and send our friends to him.

If information alone could solve financial problems, everyone would be fine; more information is available than one could read in a lifetime. No matter what information is transmitted, however, the individual needs of the person on the receiving end can't be taken into full account. Magazines, television shows, and newspapers provide investors with ideas and ideas only. Even the best research report isn't going to say, "Mr. Reader, based on your situation, you should buy five hundred shares of General Mills."

People need someone to sift through all the available ideas to find the best solutions to their specific financial problems. Who can they go to? Bankers, lawyers, and accountants may be able to point in a certain direction but are not trained to make specific investment decisions. A good financial planner can provide an overall financial roadmap, but that's merely a starting point. There's a big difference between telling someone he should be investing in growth stocks and telling him exactly what stocks in exactly what amounts and then continually monitoring the performance of those stocks for him. Clearly, stockbrokers who make full use of the resources available to them are in the best position to help people solve their financial problems.

No wonder that successful stockbrokers view themselves first and foremost as financial problem solvers. As Bob Cranshaw says, "People hire me to isolate their needs. Then it's just a matter of placing the right investments where they're needed." The opportunity open to good financial problem solvers like Bob is tremendous. The demand for their product far exceeds the existing supply.

YOUR PRODUCT: QUALITY PERSONALIZED INVESTMENT DECISIONS

How can you succeed as a financial problem solver? You can succeed by taking the same basic product that every good professional problem solver offers—a quality personalized decision—and adapting it to your field. Your basic product is *quality personalized investment decisions* or *QPID*.

By offering quality personalized investment decisions to investors you'll not only have a product that's in great demand, but one with a value that far exceeds its cost. In the long run, good investment advice, regardless of its initial cost, is the least expensive. Having a low-cost product that's in great demand—what a way to start out in business!

Let's examine more closely the four elements of QPID to see what they really mean to you and your customers.

Quality. Nobody expects you as a broker to be right all the time. That's impossible. However, at the very least you are expected to be right much more often than you are wrong. This won't happen if you toss a coin or just take a stab at something. Quality decisions—those that have the greatest probability of being the right decisions—are the result of quality input. Only if you make effective use of the resources available to you will your customers come out ahead.

Personalized. Your solutions should fit each individual customer like a well-tailored suit. The better you understand a customer's situation, the better you'll be able to solve her problems. Dollars and cents are only one aspect of a customer's situation. Thoughts, feelings, and experiences make each customer unique. Along with the calculations, you need to provide compassion. To truly serve the customer, you have to serve the person.

Investment. Investments are your area of expertise, your raison d'être. The greater your expertise, the better the job you can do for your customers. Knowledge is the foundation of professionalism.

Decisions. Investors don't want to be presented with an array of alternatives. They want decisions. Advice that stops short of telling the customer exactly what to do is nothing more than a list of ideas. Ideas are a dime a dozen.

YOU'RE CHAIRMAN OF THE BOARD

Asking two different customers of the same brokerage firm for their opinions of the firm could remind you of the tale of the blind men and the elephant. You might hear two widely different descriptions of the same animal:

> CUSTOMER ONE: "Outstanding! Huxley Buckley Securities really know what they're talking about. They take the time to make sure that the investments I make are right for me. I've sent my friends to them."
>
> CUSTOMER TWO: "Terrible! Huxley Buckley Securities got me mixed up in some investments I don't understand and I don't think they do either. I'll never give them another cent."

We can tell immediately that the customers aren't describing the elephant, Huxley Buckley Securities. Each customer is talking about the part of Huxley Buckley he's had contact with—his individual broker.

Your firm provides you with raw materials: investments, information, and services. It's up to you to turn them into a finished product. Regardless of the size, reputation, and efforts of your firm, the value of your product is ultimately your responsibility. You're the chairman of the board of your business. Look at it the way Valerie Freeman does. "I look at my business in the same fashion as the head of IBM looks at his . . . just on a slightly smaller scale."

Now, we're going to look harder at the first element of QPID: quality.

5

THE QUALITY FACTOR: IT'S NO ACCIDENT

What is it about investing that makes it so challenging? There is a very real possibility that what you think you see and what you actually get will be two entirely different things.

When you buy a new car, you can be certain that whatever model you buy will take you where you want to go for a few years. But what if your new Chevrolet wasn't going to stay a Chevrolet—after a year it was going to turn into either a Rolls-Royce or a pile of rocks? What if there was a chance that when you got behind the wheel, the car wouldn't take you where you wanted to go, even though it worked fine for your neighbor? If you couldn't find out what you were really driving out of the showroom, you'd probably keep your money in your pocket and stick to walking.

This is the kind of situation every investor faces. Investing isn't like picking something out of a catalog. What looks like a great investment might end up being a garbage disposal for money.

What's a perfectly good investment for your neighbor may be all wrong for you.

As economic, technological, and political events in the world unfold, the performance of each and every type of investment is affected in some way. The combined force of all these events creates major trends in the performance of investments. Depending on the direction of these trends, a specific investment can be lucrative one year and a loser the next. The important question is which it will be.

Let's see what impact a recent trend might have had on you (or someone you know). In November 1984, money market funds—a "day-to-day" investment with fluctuating rates—were paying over 11 percent. "Not bad for not having to tie your money up," you might have thought. A major trend was already in motion, however: interest rates were falling. One year later, in November 1985, money market funds were paying around 7½ percent. If you hadn't made a move, your savings would have taken over a 30 percent cut in return.

What could you have done about it? If you were aware of the trend, you could have done a great deal. By shifting your funds from your day-to-day money market fund to a long-term high quality bond, you would have locked in a yield slightly higher than the 11 percent your money market fund was paying. No matter how low interest rates fell, your bond would have paid over 11 percent. Also, your bond would have appreciated in value at least another 11 percent. The net result—over a 22 percent return—would have been a 100 percent increase in return on your savings, instead of a 30 percent cut. Think how helpful a stockbroker who steered you in this direction would have been. (Note that this is not a "best case" scenario, only a modest example. The decline in interest rates that began in June 1984 has made much greater gains possible.)

The key to making winning investments lies in being able to identify major trends before they become obvious to most investors and then staying with the trend, disregarding the little ups and downs along the way. In the long run, investors who exercise patience profit more than investors who chase after a quick buck.

You can't identify major investment trends by reading the paper and reacting to yesterday's news, however. You have to peer ahead into the future, far past the shortsighted view of most investors. When the crowd is clamoring to hop onto the bandwagon of an investment, you should be hopping off with a nice profit.

August 1982 saw the beginning of a major uptrend in the stock market. In the months that followed there were many times when it appeared that the stock market was in anything but an uptrend. By February 1986, however, the stock market (as measured by the Dow Jones Industrial Average) had more than doubled in value. Investors who had gotten on board and hadn't let a bump in the road throw them off were enjoying a very profitable ride. The crowd of frenzied latecomers willing to pay anything for a seat on the bandwagon hadn't even formed yet.

Even worse than missing out on making money is losing money. Being caught on the wrong side of a trend can be disastrous. Just ask anyone who invested in oil wells when the price of oil was $35 a barrel and thought to be headed to $100. The uptrend in oil prices was actually over. With oil selling currently at around $15 a barrel, many investors are less wealthy but a little wiser.

A losing investment never solved anybody's problem. No matter what a customer's need is, the solution has to be right for the times to be right for the customer. That's why successful brokers recognize the importance of identifying major investment trends and planning their business around them.

SECRET OF SIX-FIGURE SUCCESS NUMBER ONE: ALWAYS HAVE AN INVESTMENT PLAN

A good football coach never takes his team into a game without having a well-thought-out game plan. He knows that a good game plan increases his team's chances of walking off the field with a victory. A good stockbroker never walks into his office without a well-thought-out investment plan. He knows that a good investment plan safeguards his customers' chances.

Valerie Freeman explains her approach this way. "I always have an investment plan. If you don't have one, you're in trouble.

In many ways I view my business as a department store. I plan for the season ahead and make sure that I have a variety of quality merchandise on the shelves—something for everyone. You can't go digging around in the stockroom at the last minute and hope that you'll find the right thing every time you sit down with a customer."

An investment plan is the road map that guides your investment decisions. It is the result of carefully studying the past and the present and then developing the most likely scenario for the future. An investment plan identifies major investment trends, the specific investments that will best take advantage of those trends, and the investments to avoid.

No matter what the needs of the customer, an investment plan will point you toward the right solution. Every customer is unique, but every customer lives in the same world. Understanding what's going on in the world will enable you to guide each one.

How will an investment plan increase your success? Here are three ways:

1. Better Investment Decisions Successful investing is based on anticipation and action, not observation and reaction. You should be ahead of the crowd, not trying to catch up with it. A good investment plan will guide you toward attractive investment opportunities before they become generally apparent and will give you the conviction to stick with them.

Decisions based on emotion or impulse are usually wrong. Anyone who purchased gold at $800 an ounce will attest to that. Your investment plan will restrain you from joining the emotional stampedes that always leave thousands of unhappy investors in their wake.

A successful broker at Wheat, First Securities feels that his investment plan made the big difference in his career. "Several years ago when I started telling people that interest rates were going to go way down, they looked at me like I was crazy. But when I explained why, it made sense, and they took action on my recommendations. When you make your clients money like that, it comes back to you many times over."

2. Increased Self-Confidence   In a business where each day you have to introduce yourself to scores of new people and make many important decisions, the value of having confidence in your knowledge and abilities cannot be overestimated. There is no substitute for the feeling that comes from knowing what you're talking about. (You'll find out how really important this is in the next two chapters.)

3. Increased Business   Walk into a brokerage office after the stock market has been in a downtrend for a while. You'll hear brokers moaning, "I haven't done any business for days. This market is killing me." The broker who has an investment plan won't be part of this chorus. Why not? She knows that change brings opportunity and uses her investment plan to direct her toward that opportunity.

If the stock market is down, perhaps bonds or mutual funds specializing in foreign stocks are a good buy. By working with the broad spectrum of available investments, you'll have a steadier and greater stream of business. There's always opportunity somewhere. An investment plan will help you find it.

How can you put together an investment plan when you're just starting out? The greatest teacher is the one thing you have the least of—experience. You have to go out and draw on the experience of others.

CHOOSING YOUR PERSONAL ADVISORY BOARD, OR HOW TO AVOID "PARALYSIS BY ANALYSIS"

Every brokerage office manager can tell a story of a new broker who spent so much time trying to figure out what to do that in the end he did nothing and was soon out of business. It's easy to become a victim of "paralysis by analysis." There are thousands of viewpoints on every investment topic, and each one comes from someone with an important-sounding title. (The rarest title on Wall Street is NAVP—"Not a Vice-President.") Trying to be a poll-taker results in a game of mental Ping-Pong and few decisions. As for quality, if you've ever been on a committee you know that excellence is usually compromised by numbers.

Your job is to make decisions that address the needs of your clients effectively. This doesn't include starting from scratch with a pile of data and deriving conclusions about the financial markets. That's a full-time job that belongs to someone else—an investment analyst.

Like any other professionals, some investment analysts are better than others. Since your goal is quality, there's no need to follow the advice of all of them. Just choose the best. By carefully selecting two or three top investment analysts and using their research as the basis for your investment plan, you'll be taking full advantage of the best resources available. The result will be that your personal advisory board will comprise some of the top investment minds in the world.

Successful brokers know that the quality of their investment plan is critical. But they also realize that the more time they spend putting it together, the less time they have to run their businesses. Making use of the best research available eliminates both concerns. It is both efficient and effective.

As your career progresses, your own experience and knowledge will play an expanding role in the creation of your investment plan. Even the most experienced veterans, however, carefully follow several analysts, as a fast-track broker at Shearson Lehman Brothers discovered. He says, "When I started out, I went around to the brokers who had reputations as being savvy investors and discovered that one of their secrets was the research analysts they followed. That saved me a lot of trial and error."

Here are a few tips on selecting research analysts for your advisory board.

1. Don't confuse ego with excellence. We tend to be drawn toward loud, confident opinions. Good analysts realize though that investment choices are rarely spelled out in black and white; they are based on shades of gray. Look for analysts who spend their time trying to watch the

financial markets for clues to the future. The financial markets don't listen to those who try to tell *them* what to do. A good analyst uses "probable" far more often than "definite."

2. Put your money on the tortoise. When you evaluate the performance of an analyst, keep in mind that the key to a good track record is consistency. This year's sensations have a tendency to be next year's disasters. The analyst who consistently takes you a step forward each year will take you much further than the speedster who keeps sending you back to the starting line.

3. Don't leave your chair. You should be able to find out what your analysts are thinking without running around. Choose analysts whose reports can come directly to you, with as little delay as possible. Your research time should be spent reading, not trying to find out someone's opinion.

4. Look in your own back yard. Don't overlook your firm's research department. It has always amazed me that a top analyst can be respected by everyone on Wall Street except the brokers at his own firm. The grass may appear to be greener somewhere else, but chances are that your own back yard may have what you're looking for.

SECRET OF SIX-FIGURE SUCCESS NUMBER TWO: BUY LOW-RISK, HIGH-QUALITY INVESTMENTS

Your investment plan is like an architect's plan; it's only on paper. You now have to select the materials, the specific investments that will best help you to implement your strategy. Whatever direction your investment plan takes, choose low-risk, high-quality investments.

Richard Desiderio feels that quality is an essential ingredient in successful investing. "I believe in buying quality and being patient. With those two factors, you'll ultimately be rewarded. I don't think anyone who trades in and out of risky investments is ever going to win in the long run."

Quite simply, quality means dependability. Every investor alive would like to own part of the next IBM or the company that finds a cure for cancer, but the odds of finding these companies are very low. The well-managed company that makes a "boring" product—and more and more money every year—may not seem exciting, but over a period of time it will prove to be a better investment than ninety-nine out of one hundred of the gambles that mistakenly get called investments.

Here are some reasons why high-quality investments will help you build a solid business.

1. They Are a Surer Path to Profits In a time when coverage of investment windfalls shares headlines with instant lottery millionaires, it's easy to lose sight of the fact that the most money is made by investors who carefully select quality investments and patiently stick with them.

People don't expect you to double their money in a year; you'll only lose money if you try. A portfolio manager who achieves a 15 percent return year-in, year-out over an extended period of time will rank with the best in the profession. There are plenty of quality investments that can put you in that circle. Don't overlook the power of compound interest. An investment that returns 12 percent, compounded annually, will double in six years. Most people would be happy with that kind of performance from their investments. There's no sense gambling to attain the virtually unattainable when a conservative approach is likely to deliver satisfactory results.

When you buy and hold quality investments, sooner or later some will double or even triple in value, without your having taken undue risk. This is the kind of investment that an investor never forgets; neither does she forget the broker who made the recommendation.

2. Everyone Sleeps Better Despite what they may say beforehand, most people (including most brokers) aren't suited emotionally to deal with the "fast lane" of speculative investing. Nine times out of ten an investor will blame you when he loses money on a speculative investment, even if it wasn't your idea in the first place. Instead of making financial decisions, you'll be running the complaint department. Before too long you'll be avoiding your own customers, if they're not already avoiding you. Low-risk quality investments help your customers sleep, since they know their money will be there in the morning. They also help you sleep, since you know your customers will be there in the morning.

3. Quality Doesn't Need a Babysitter Speculative investments take up too much valuable time. Not only do you need to watch them constantly, but you'll also spend time holding your customers' hands. Quality investments allow you to spend time expanding your business instead of babysitting.

BUILDING YOUR INVENTORY

After the deregulation of commissions in 1975, brokerage firms began looking for new sources of revenue. The result was that they began to offer a wider variety of investments to their customers. In an effort to capture as much of the investor's dollar as possible, brokerage firms may now offer as many as 150 different investments, with the number climbing every week.

There's no way that you can start your business knowing about every possible investment alternative, but there are a number of products basic to your business that you'll learn about during your training. Once you get started, you'll continue to master additional investments.

It's not enough to have a working knowledge of your inventory, however. You should be an absolute expert on it. Once you've said that you know about an investment, having to say that you don't know damages your credibility. "I won't pick up my phone unless I'm certain that I know all the basics of the investment I'm going to talk about," a rising broker with A. G. Edwards and Sons affirms. "If I can't answer an obvious question, the person isn't going to listen to another word I say."

To stay competitive you have to stay up to date and well informed. This not only means keeping your investment plan current, it also means learning about any new investments offered by your firm. The larger your inventory of solutions, the greater the service you can offer to your customers.

You can be certain that if a new investment requires an evening or two of study, most of your competition has already dropped it. Spend the time. Many of the areas brokerage firms are expanding into, such as insurance and banking services, can be appropriate no matter what the financial climate. Also, demonstrating knowledge in new areas is an excellent way to enhance your professional image.

Now you've done enough "homework." It's time to open your doors for business.

6
PROSPECTING: HOW TO FIND CUSTOMERS

You'll begin your first day in business in the same situation as every other stockbroker has. You'll have a desk, a phone, a quote machine, and no customers. For a moment you may feel like a tourist standing on the edge of the Grand Canyon. You stand on one side with all your knowledge and enthusiasm. On the other side of a large gap stand a lot of people you haven't met yet: your potential customers.

You may be tempted to wait for customers to come to you. You'll soon find out that when you're new in the business very few customers will walk through your door. You may look at your family and friends and think that their business will be enough to make you successful. Unless your last name is Rockefeller, don't delude yourself.

To succeed you are going to have to bridge the gap between you and your potential customers. You are going to have to introduce yourself. It's the only way that people are going to know who you are and what you have to offer. Looking for customers is called *prospecting*.

If you took a survey of first-year stockbrokers, asking what they liked least about their jobs, the most frequent answer would be "prospecting." Working with people and with investments is fun. Introducing yourself to people you don't know and trying to strike up conversations about their financial situations for the purpose of doing business is another story.

Successful stockbrokers love prospecting, however. They're not superhuman or masochistic. They'd probably rather be doing just about anything else, but successful brokers realize that prospecting is what makes their ever-increasing incomes possible.

Your firm is relying on you and your fellow brokers to bring customers in. There isn't a single brokerage firm that can survive on advertising alone. The most effective way for a firm to get customers is through the prospecting efforts of its brokers.

If prospecting were easy, brokers would be paid a modest salary and you wouldn't be reading this book. Since not everyone can prospect, the rewards for those who can are unlimited. Your clients reward you for quality. Your firm pays you for quantity.

There are two inescapable principles that apply to prospecting for new accounts.

1. *There is a direct relationship between the number of new accounts you open and your level of success.*

At any firm, at any level of experience, the most successful brokers are also the leaders in opening new accounts—attracting new customers. Your ability to open new accounts will be the single most important factor in your success. How many new accounts will it take to achieve your goal of earning $100,000? There are several variables involved. The size of the accounts you open—how much money the customers have to invest—is one variable. Your skill in developing your accounts—cultivating and expanding your business with each customer—is another. You should open at least 500 accounts over your first three years. Even this number as a bare minimum doesn't guarantee success. Far better is to aim for opening an average of one new account every business day, or approximately 250 a year. Don't be discouraged by that number. The top brokers at most firms open 400 or more new accounts a year!

2. *There is a direct relationship between the number of potential customers you talk to each day and the number of new accounts you open.*

Prospecting is a numbers game. The more potential customers you actually talk to each day, the more customers you'll end up with. Prospecting is really your personal advertising campaign. People can't buy a product they don't know about. It's up to you to make as many people as possible aware of how you can be of service to them.

If two brokers have equal skills and experience, but one talks to twenty good prospects a day and the other to forty, you can be sure the latter broker opens more new accounts. There is simply no substitute for exposure.

How many prospects will you have to contact each day? Let's say that your goal is to open one new account each business day. An average of one out of ten prospects will indicate any interest in working with you. Of these, at best half will eventually open an account. That's only one out of twenty of your initial contacts. If you want to open 250 new accounts a year, you'll have to contact over 5,000 prospective customers. When you add the fact that it usually takes four or five conversations before a prospect opens an account, you can easily see that you are going to have to talk to an awful lot of people to be successful.

THE MOST IMPORTANT TOOL OF THE TRADE: THE TELEPHONE

There's no way that you can contact several hundred people a week without an efficient method. That's why the patron saint of successful stockbrokers is Alexander Graham Bell. The telephone is the most important tool of the trade.

The telephone enables you to perform amazing feats. You can cover great distances instantly, without leaving your office. The phone allows you to talk with many different people in a short

period of time. It takes you right to the person you want to talk
to in seconds. Using the telephone may seem impersonal, but it
doesn't have to be. You can make it more personal.

The telephone is also a great equalizer. It guarantees that no
one has too much of a head start in the numbers game. With a
telephone and hard work, it's possible for a twenty-one-year-old
college graduate who just moved to an area to build a more
successful business than that of a well-connected lifelong resident
twice his age. The telephone helps a broker open doors and meet
people quickly. No matter who you are or where you work, you
will have a phone; and a broker at the smallest firm in town can
be more successful than any of her counterparts at the major
firms if she out-prospects them.

Prospecting by telephone, or "cold calling," is the predominant
method of prospecting used by successful brokers to build their
businesses, especially in the first several years of their careers.
It's not that other means of prospecting don't work. Seminars,
knocking on doors, mailings, and involvement in civic activities
can be effective. But the broker is in a small minority who builds
a successful business using methods that don't include cold calling. More often these alternatives are used by successful brokers
to supplement their phone efforts.

A Smith Barney manager sums up the importance of cold
calling this way: "The broker who tells me that cold calling doesn't
work for him usually hasn't worked at it and usually ends up out
of work. The exceptions are far outnumbered by the failures."
The following comments from successful brokers, all of whom
hit the six-figure income level in less than three years, back this
up.

"The telephone is number one—I want to contact as many
people as I can get to."

"Ninety percent of my prospecting is by phone."

"Cold calling helped me get in doors that otherwise would have
been closed."

PHONE FEAR: HOW TO OVERCOME IT

Given how well cold calling has been proven by successful brokers to be a path to the top, it's incredible how many new brokers do everything but pick up the phone. It's not that they've found a better way to prospect or that they don't understand the importance of prospecting. They simply act as though their phones were made of lead.

You'll hear a thousand and one reasons from brokers in your office for why they aren't picking up the phone and prospecting. Very few have anything to do with the truth. "I don't have time," "I'm tired of prospecting," or "Everyone I call is out to lunch, in a meeting, or on vacation" are really cover-ups for something else: a voice inside them that says "I'd rather do anything in the world than pick up the phone." That feeling can stop the career of a broker dead in its tracks. I've watched brokers who felt at home speaking to an audience of hundreds freeze when it was time to pick up the phone.

Whenever I ask a group of new brokers, "What's the biggest barrier to picking up the phone?" the overwhelming response is "fear of rejection." I certainly agree that not many of us relish the idea of getting shot down repeatedly day after day. I believe, however, that there is another barrier to picking up the phone in addition to the fear of rejection, one that I've sensed in many of the new brokers I've worked with: a negative self-image. Let's look at this first.

NEGATIVE SELF-IMAGE

Most people's watchword in life is *improvement*, physical, financial, mental, and spiritual. When you become a stockbroker you become a respected professional in a dynamic field with unlimited earnings potential. But if you're not careful, your mind will play tricks on you and make you feel like someone entirely different.

Think for a moment about telephone solicitors. You envision irritating people who call you at inconvenient times to try to sell you something, usually by reading a script in an impersonal monotone until you can get them off the phone. Do you welcome their calls? Do you sit by the telephone waiting for someone to sell you a magazine subscription or aluminum siding? Of course not. Phone solicitors rank with bill collectors in the "how could anyone do that for a living and still look at himself in the mirror" category for many people.

On the surface a stockbroker has a lot in common with a telephone solicitor. You both use the telephone to find customers. You both call people you've never met. You both want something from the people you call. If you think this way, it will be easy for you to feel like a telephone solicitor instead of a professional financial advisor when you prospect. How much are you going to want to do something that you hate having done to you? After all, if people were really interested, they'd call you.

To be successful, you must look at yourself entirely differently: as a professional with the desire and know-how to affect people's lives positively.

Bob Cranshaw gives an example of how he's helped a customer: "I opened an account last year with a fellow—I'll call him Mr. Jones—who had $25,000 that had been sitting for years in a savings account earning 5¼ percent. Nobody from the bank had ever called him about investing it at a higher rate. I doubled his return overnight. One year later, he still hasn't stopped thanking me. Why? Because I'm putting an extra $1,300 a year in his pocket. When you're retired, that can make a big difference."

There are millions of Mr. and Mrs. Joneses out there. If you've done your homework, you should never feel the slightest bit insecure about prospecting. You are offering a product that people want and need. You're ready, willing, and able to help people with a crucial element of their lives, their financial well-being. Why not feel good about it? Walk into your office thinking, "There are people out there who need me, and I'm going to find them." It's all in your attitude.

Think about the times you've volunteered to help raise money for a local charity, for example, the local children's hospital. You had a very good feeling about what you were doing. Your confidence in your work made asking people for contributions easy. They benefitted too, from the knowledge that their donations were helping to improve the quality of their community. Thinking "I'm just calling to help myself" helps to foster a negative self-image. You want everyone to be a winner.

FEAR OF REJECTION

Picture a baseball game. It's the bottom of the ninth with two out and the winning run on second base. The best hitter on the team, a Hall of Fame candidate with a .300 career batting average, steps to the plate. Is he afraid of making an out? If he stopped for a moment and thought about it, he'd realize that even with his exceptional record he only has a three-in-ten chance of delivering the game-winning hit. The 40,000 cheering fans are likely to be going home disappointed in a few minutes. How come his eyes are filled with determination, not fear? Because he has understood the odds of being successful since the day he first picked up a bat. He knows that his failures will always outnumber his successes; but if he gets enough chances, those successes will mount up.

Of all the potential customers you contact each day, about 10 percent will show an interest in what you have to offer. That means if you're a .100 hitter on your initial contacts, you're an all-star. If you can convert a significant percentage of those interested prospects into customers, you're going to end up in the Stockbroker Hall of Fame. So why let all the strike-outs bother you? If you don't take your swings and sometimes strike out, you won't open any accounts.

No matter how effective a prospector you become, you're going to be rejected far more times than not. The people you're calling don't know you, so there's no reason to take it personally when they say "no thank you." Many of the reasons for the "no thank you's" are beyond your control. For instance:

- There are people who so dislike receiving cold calls that they will not want to listen to you, no matter how professionally you approach them.
- There are people who are simply not in the position to take advantage of your services. If you were selling cars,

would it bother you if a person who didn't drive said no?
- You may have just caught a person at a bad time. How could you possibly know, unless you have X-ray vision, that when you call, someone's boss is waiting outside their office for a report that was due yesterday, or that their most valuable customer is on the other line? In a Merrill Lynch office in Atlanta, different brokers tried repeatedly to prospect one of the wealthiest individuals in town with no success. Finally, one of the newest brokers in the office opened the account. He had simply called at 5:30 P.M. on a Friday, and the prospect had the time to talk.

Even knowing in advance that it's going to happen doesn't completely eliminate the sting of a succession of no's. But there's another feeling that's far worse: the feeling of not having enough customers to sustain a successful business. Any broker who has experienced this will tell you that it's the worst, most helpless feeling in the business.

If you're worried about the doors that are closed, you'll never find the ones that are open. An E. F. Hutton broker looks at it this way: "Every 'no' brings me one step closer to a 'yes.'" There are people in your area waiting to do business with you. You'll never find them unless you keep trying. As the number of your customers multiplies, the rejection you experience along the way will be completely buried by an avalanche of satisfaction.

ONE STEP AT A TIME

There's more to being a good prospector than just picking up the phone and dialing. As with any endeavor, you can't be successful unless you know what you're trying to accomplish. Goals are achieved one step at a time. If you try to jump from start to finish in one leap, chances are good that you'll fall on your face.

When you call a prospect, your ultimate goal is to do business. You want the prospect to become your customer. Why not skip the formalities, then, and launch right into a sales pitch? Well, if you don't want to seem like a magazine salesman, don't act like one.

You cannot offer a solution unless you know the problem. You can't determine the problem if you're trying to sell something the minute you get a prospect on the line. How would you feel if you went to the doctor and, before you had a chance to say two words, he handed you some pills and said "Take these"? You'd turn around and hi-tail it out of his office. Before you can make any recommendations, you need to know some things about the prospect. Remember what the *P* stands for in QPID—*personalized*.

Can you call prospects and just start reeling off a list of questions about their finances? You can try—but would you answer a list of questions from a complete stranger about your money? Of course not. Your objective may be to gather information about the prospect, but dead phone lines don't talk, only willing prospects do.

Your immediate goal when you pick up the phone is to start a conversation with the prospect. You are on a fact-finding mission. Unless the prospect talks to you, his phone number will be the first and last fact you ever find out about him.

OPENING THE CALL: MAKING YOUR FIRST IMPRESSION

The first fifteen seconds of a prospecting call are in many ways the most important. You don't want them to be also the last fifteen seconds of the call. Your introduction, or "opener," shouldn't be chosen haphazardly. You'll be using it to introduce yourself to scores of new people each day. You want to make the right first impression.

Every successful broker will tell you that there's only one opener that works: the opener he or she uses. In reality, there's no magic opener. What matters is not so much what you use, it's how often you use it. The more comfortable your opener makes you feel, the easier it is to pick up the phone. Your opener is like the clothes you wear to work. Whether your style is Brooks Brothers or green polyester, if you feel good about what you're wearing, you're going to feel more natural and confident. The more relaxed and self-assured an image you convey to prospects, the greater the likelihood that they'll want to talk to you.

The number of prospecting calls you make is more important than the words you use in your opener. You must recognize, however, that your opener has a tough job to do. It has to shift the prospect's attention from whatever he's in the middle of when you call, overcome his initial impulse to get you off the phone as fast as possible, and start a conversation about the prospect's investment situation. Although that's a tall order for a couple of sentences, there are several ways you can increase the effectiveness of your opener.

1. Offer the prospect a potential benefit for talking with you. Let the prospect know you are trying to be of service to him, not sell him something.
2. Make your opener clear and concise. It should be no more than two sentences long; leave the monologues to Johnny Carson. Don't use big words or Wall Street jargon. You want to communicate, not confuse.
3. Involve the prospect as soon as possible. If you want the prospect to talk, make sure that you give him a chance. Make your introduction, ask the prospect a question about himself, zip your lips, and listen.

Don't take the first hint of "no" from a prospect as a signal to beat a retreat. It may very well be a reflex response to a cold call. Relax. Offer another benefit, and ask the prospect another question. If you act professional, the prospect is more likely to think, "Hey, wait a minute. Maybe this person can help me."

Keep in mind that on average nine out of ten cold calls will stay cold and will end quickly. Don't try to talk every prospect into submission. Concentrate instead on fanning the sparks of interest that you kindle into conversations.

WHAT YOU NEED TO KNOW ABOUT A PROSPECT AND HOW TO FIND IT OUT

To get an accurate picture of prospects, that will identify their problems and help you prescribe the right solutions, you need to gather information in four basic areas. They are:

1. What are her goals? Where does the prospect want to go? Different people want their money to do different things for them. Your recommendations for a forty-three-year-old business owner concerned with having her money grow may be entirely different from your recommendations for a fifty-eight-year-old executive planning for his retirement.
2. What is her current situation? What is she doing to achieve her goals, if anything? You can't write a prescription unless you know the current state of the patient.
3. Who's helping her now, if anyone? You can't compete for her business unless you know whom you're competing against.
4. How much money does she have to invest? You simply cannot make the right recommendation unless you know what you have to work with. This is the one question that new brokers have the toughest time asking, but it's impossible to be a professional and not ask it.

One of the keys to starting a conversation is simply remembering that everybody's favorite topic of conversation is himself. Why not oblige? Questions that begin with "what," "why," and "how" give a prospect the chance to open up. The less you talk during a prospecting call, the better. Don't ask strings of questions that allow for only one- or two-word responses. You want the prospect to get involved, not just be a backboard for a game of Twenty Questions.

You are going to be asking a prospect some very personal questions. You can't expect too many answers unless you show the prospect some benefits of answering your questions. One way to look at a prospecting call is as a trading session. You are trading information about the potential benefits of the prospect's becoming your customer for information about himself. Don't expect to be able to make too many one-sided deals. You have to provide some good answers to "What's in this for me?"

A good benefit statement tells the prospect only what he needs to know, not everything you know. You are making the prospect aware that you have solutions, but you will need to know more about the prospect before you know which solution is best for him. Stating potential benefits does more than help you learn about the prospect. It motivates the prospect to work with you to solve his problems. Benefits can turn a cold call into a partnership.

Benefits are your greatest ally, as a student of mine found out one minute into his first prospecting call. The call went like this:

> **BROKER:** "How are you currently investing your money?"
> **PROSPECT** (politely but coolly): "It's in the bank."
> **BROKER:** "How much do you currently have invested there?"
> **PROSPECT** (snapping): "What business is it of yours?"
> **BROKER:** "Well, how high a return I could get for you would depend in part on how much you invest."
> **PROSPECT** (suddenly broker's long-lost best friend): "Why, two hundred thousand dollars."

It isn't always this easy, but unless you give people a reason to talk to you, they won't.

PROSPECTS ARE PEOPLE TOO

Never forget that on the other end of the phone line is a real person, not a voice with a seven-digit identification number guarding a pile of money. The more you try to identify with the individual behind the voice and phone number, the greater the chances that the prospect will want to do business with you.

Prospecting is a "people" skill. Don't be afraid to inject some personality into the proceedings. Believe it or not, most of your customers will tend to be similar to you in personality. You can't be all things to all people, so you might as well be yourself. Being a serious professional doesn't mean that you have to be a stiff.

Prospecting is a skill best learned through experience, but repetition is only part of your learning. Take the time to reflect on what you're doing. When a call doesn't go your way, put yourself in the prospect's shoes and ask yourself, "How could I have been more effective?" You can't expect people to respond in a certain way if you wouldn't if you were in the same situation.

DON'T BEAT YOUR HEAD AGAINST THE WALL

It will usually take quite a few calls to a prospect to open the account. Remember, however, it's not your job to open an account with everyone, so don't try. If you're making progress with a prospect and each call brings you closer to opening an account, keep at it. If you're spinning your wheels, your time will be better spent calling new prospects.

Not everyone is qualified to take advantage of your services. Investing requires money. That's why you need to ask tough questions. Otherwise, you might prospect someone for months only to find out that he only has $100 to his name. Don't just look at today, though. The prospect could be in the same situation you're in—on his way to success but not quite there. It would be better to establish a relationship now than vie for the prospect's business in a few years along with ten other brokers.

THE CONTRACT: DON'T SIGN OFF WITHOUT IT

Never end a conversation with a prospect with whom you'll be speaking again without clearly establishing a mutually agreed-upon time, date, and place for your next call. There are two good reasons for this.

1. The prospect will be expecting your call. No longer will you be a cold caller from out of the blue. This helps the prospect perceive you as a member of his team.
2. It forces you to follow up. Too often a call that ends with "I'll get back to you sometime" gets lost in the shuffle, and "sometime" becomes "never."

FACE TO FACE: WHERE MORE BUSINESS TAKES PLACE

Using the phone is the most efficient way to talk to people. The most *effective* way is face-to-face. Just because your initial contact with a prospect is by telephone doesn't mean that you're restricted to the phone.

There's no doubt that you can build greater rapport with a prospect, get more information, and set the stage for doing more business by meeting her. Start with the phone, but aim for an appointment. As Ken Latham explains, "Appointments are essential. It adds the personal touch to a business that's so much a numbers game." We'll discuss the role of appointments in building a successful business further in the next chapter.

WHO TO CALL

Picking up the phone is the first step in becoming a good prospector. But not so fast. Who are you going to call? If you just call anyone, you could end up wasting a tremendous amount of time talking to people who can't use your services.

The quantity of your prospecting calls is extremely important, but the quality of the people you call isn't far behind. It's as if you were a prospector in the Gold Rush. It won't matter how hard you work if the creek bed you're digging in is mined out or never had gold to begin with. You can improve your prospecting efforts considerably by spending a little time beforehand on your list of prospects.

Let's use Broker A and Broker B as examples of the difference this can make. They both spend the morning prospecting by telephone.

Broker A opens the telephone book and starts dialing. He spends most of the morning calling disconnected numbers, "nobody-homes," soap-opera fans, the unemployed, and people who don't even have a vague idea of what a stockbroker is. By noon Broker A has a headache and one mediocre lead to show for his efforts.

Broker B spent her lunch hour yesterday over at the city courthouse. She wrote down the names of everyone who had purchased or sold real estate in the last month. Her reasoning was that the people who had bought might be new to the area and the people who had sold might have cash to invest.

Broker B is calling the people on her list. Sure, she gets a good many "no thank you's." By the end of the morning, however, she has an appointment with a corporate executive who was just transferred into town; an investor is sending her a $100,000 check received from the sale of a building, to invest in bonds; and she has leads on two more potentially good customers. The smile on her face tells us her extra effort was worth it.

Not too long ago, a brokerage office manager in San Francisco called in a consultant to help solve a problem. The new brokers in the office were prospecting day and night with nothing to show for it. After a few hours, the consultant reported back to the manager. The problem was obvious—the brokers were all calling the same people. The local Chamber of Commerce directory was filled with qualified prospects, but it was also easy to obtain. The list had been prospected to death. The moral of the story is that if brokers can get a list without lifting a finger, the people on it have been prospected into the ground.

Don't agonize over every name you put on your list. You have to make calls. However, with some effort and creativity you can increase the results of your prospecting hours by improving the quality of your list. Use your imagination. Here are just a few ideas for sources to get you started:

- *Group directories.* There's a directory for just about any group or organization. Lists of businesses, college alumni, country club members, patrons of the arts, members of flying and boating clubs, parents whose children attend a private school, and civic organizations are a few possibilities.
- *Newspapers.* These are great sources, especially in smaller cities. The local business section will tell you about people who've been promoted. The society pages will tip you off to centers of wealth. Look for real estate transactions too.
- *City directories.* Many cities have directories that list people by street address and give you a person's place of employment and position there. Look in the reference section of your local library (another good source of leads).

A few additional tips on prospecting lists:

1. If you don't have the time to do the leg work to generate a list, hire someone to do it for you. One good customer will return your investment many times over. Many

brokers get spoiled by having almost everything paid for by their firms. Don't be afraid to spend money to make money.

2. Money has no dress code. It doesn't necessarily end up in the hands of people who wear white shirts and ties. Do you dread calling the plumber or the television repairman or taking your car to be fixed because you're afraid it won't cost that much? A person with a good income who doesn't care about showing it off is a better prospect than the high-salaried hotshot up to his ears in payments on a fancy home and a Mercedes.

3. Money has no sexual preference. Women own 50 percent of the stock held by individuals in this country, are getting high-paying jobs in greater numbers, and frequently are the financial decision makers in their households.

4. Good prospects don't always come by the bundle. Throughout the day, you come across good leads without even realizing it. The restaurant where you couldn't get a reservation is owned by somebody. So is the construction company that's rebuilding the road where you got tied up in traffic this morning. Keep your eyes and ears open, and your pencil and pad nearby at all times.

5. Recruit your family and friends. Get them to be "prospect conscious."

6. Get out of town. The farther away from your city you prospect, the less likely it is that you'll be tripping over other brokers' feet. Prospect the outlying areas of your territory.

SECRET OF SIX-FIGURE SUCCESS NUMBER THREE: DON'T WAIT TO GO ELEPHANT HUNTING

The trademarks of successful brokers include not only the large number of accounts they open, but also the number of big accounts: customers who generate thousands of dollars a year in business. About 80 percent of your business will come from 20 percent of your accounts. The bigger your best accounts, the more business you'll do. Why do successful brokers end up with more big accounts? They look for them.

Valerie Freeman believes the sooner a broker goes elephant hunting, the better. "I started calling the wealthiest people in my area my first day in business. They didn't bite. People with money are looking for good ideas, just like everyone else. Once you feel comfortable calling them, you can call anybody. If you wait too long, you'll never call prime prospects."

As part of my work, I've often posed the question of who to call to groups of broker trainees who are just about to start out in the business. I'm constantly dismayed at the high percentage who are saving lists of highly qualified prospects for somewhere down the line. The theory that practicing on the small fry will somehow prepare you for prospecting wealthy investors is about as valid as thinking that you can learn how to drive on a freeway by practicing in your driveway. If you want to open good accounts, call good prospects from day one. Sure you may fall down the first couple of times and skin your knees, but you can't reach the top of the learning curve until you attempt to scale it.

Often the best investors are like the prettiest girl in the senior class who doesn't get asked to the prom. Everybody thinks that somebody else has already asked. A broker friend of mine worked in a building that housed the executive offices of a "Fortune 500" corporation. When he met the chairman of its board at a social function and told him where he worked, the chairman remarked that he'd worked in the same building for ten years and had never been contacted by anyone from the broker's office. A multimillion dollar investor was just floors away, and no one had ever knocked on his door!

On your path to success, you'll work with many small investors, some of whom will eventually grow into big accounts. In order to attain a high level of success, though, you'll need a healthy number of big accounts right from the start. The only way you'll capture these elephants is by going out and trying. The sooner the better. They won't come to you.

So far you've done a lot of work, but you still don't have a cent to show for it. Now we'll talk about converting your hard work into hard dollars.

7

FROM PROSPECT TO CUSTOMER TO CLIENT: HOW TO SELL INVESTMENTS

In a very real sense you are a salesman: your income is determined by the commission dollars your business generates. This doesn't mean that you have to act like a fast-talking, pushy used-car salesman to be successful. There's no reason that you have to try to force something down someone's throat when there's a better way, for you and the customer.

If you've ever tried to fix something, you know that there's no substitute for having the right parts. When you have the right parts, the job is easy, not a frustrating day-long ordeal. Solving a financial problem is no different. If you have the right part for fixing the customer's problem, the job is easy.

So far you've focused your efforts on two areas: studying investments and learning about your prospects. When you combine the two, you will have the right parts.

THE FIRST SALE: TURNING THE PROSPECT INTO A CUSTOMER

There's only one way that a prospect can open an account and become a customer. He must make an investment. That first transaction, regardless of how much money is actually invested, is in many ways the most important. The prospect is now your customer, and you are now his broker. You are officially a team that can work to make things happen.

Opening the account is just the starting point in your relationship with the customer. Remember, many prospects will be unwilling to tell you everything there is to know about their finances. Don't get discouraged; your goal is first and foremost to open the account. Aim high, but keep in mind that you may have to cure a sore throat before a customer trusts you enough to let you perform surgery. The important thing is to get your foot in the door!

Over the course of your conversations with a prospect, you will be gathering a lot of information about the prospect's needs, goals, and current situation. Unless the prospect is one in a hundred, there are going to be some very obvious problems that need to be addressed, problems that can be easily solved with great benefit to the prospect.

The first step in opening an account is to identify a problem. It could be that the prospect has more money than necessary parked in his checking account earning an inferior interest rate; that he needs to plan for retirement; that he pays too much in taxes; or that he would like his money to grow faster. Regardless of its nature, the problem must be isolated and clearly defined before you can look for a solution.

The second step is to get the prospect to agree that a problem exists and to obtain his commitment to solving the problem. If the prospect is like most people, he will have swept his problem under the "someday I'll get around to it" rug. Richard Desiderio sees getting the problems out in the open and identified as critical. "You have to get people to understand their problems and the ramifications of not taking care of them. People can't picture six months down the road, let alone six or sixteen years. You have to spell it out for them, saying 'Here's what you're missing out on if you don't open a retirement account.'"

If you've done a good job letting the prospect know the potential benefits of working with you, he'll know that you have a range of solutions to his problem. The important question is this: if you find the right solution to the prospect's problem, is he willing to go ahead and take action, or is he going to sweep it back under the rug? A positive answer not only weeds out the window shoppers from the action takers, but it also gets the prospect psychologically ready to see himself as your customer. The relationship just needs to be formalized.

Now comes the third step: finding the right part. From the entire range of investment possibilities, the prospect's needs, objectives, and personal and financial situation will eliminate all but a handful of choices.

This is when your investment plan becomes important. It will direct you to the investment(s) that makes the most sense in the real world. Anybody can read a book and then tell someone, "If you want income, buy bonds." You get paid for deciding which bonds (or stocks or whatever). After you've selected the investments that in theory could solve the problem, use your investment plan to determine which specific investment currently offers the greatest opportunity to the investor.

Once you've selected the right investment, the finish line is in sight. Two more steps, and you're in the winner's circle.

HOW TO PRESENT AN INVESTMENT RECOMMENDATION

Whether you're making a recommendation to a prospect or to someone you've been doing business with for years, the guidelines are the same. The key to presenting an investment recommendation effectively is to remember who you are and what the main interest of your customer is.

You are a professional. If you've done your homework, there's no need to include everything you know in justifying your recommendation. You will not impress the customer; you will only confuse him, put him to sleep, or make him question your self-confidence. He already assumes that you know your stuff. If he has a question, he'll ask it. Look at it this way. Have you ever had a doctor describe the chemical structure of aspirin to you? Do you really care?

Your customer is interested in one thing: results. He wants to know how this investment is going to solve his specific problem. The more you relate the benefits of the investment to the customer's situation, the more motivated the customer will be to take action. The power to overcome the customer's inertia has to come from somewhere. If you supply the right benefits, the customer will supply most of the energy.

An investment presentation should be brief and to the point. What you say is more important than how much you say. Your presentation should answer three basic questions:

- What is your recommendation and what need does it address?
- Why have you selected it?
- How will it solve the customer's problem?

For most investments, this should take no more than a couple of minutes.

Be very careful to avoid making your presentation in "brokerese." Put it in English. During a presentation is not the time to show off the important-sounding phrases you learned while studying for the GSE, and numbers don't mean a thing unless you can tie them to a benefit. The customer might not understand "earnings per share growth rate," but will have no problem responding to the idea of a company making more and more money every year.

While you're prospecting, listening is your most important job. The investment presentation is your time to take the floor, but this doesn't mean you should stop listening. The customer may raise some questions or objections. No matter how insignificant they may seem to you, you have to respond to them satisfactorily. If it's important to the customer, it's important to you.

There will be times during a presentation when it may become clear that your recommendation isn't quite on target. Don't try to bulldoze the customer; go back to the drawing board with the new information in hand. You'll get the business; you will just get it tomorrow instead of today. The real key to getting business is in the fifth and final step.

ASKING FOR THE ORDER

Remember what the *D* stands for in QPID—*decisions.* Unless you tell the customer exactly what to do and when to do it, you're just another voice in the investment wilderness, calling out another idea. You've provided the motivation for the customer to take action. Now you have to make taking action as easy as possible.

Like all successful stockbrokers, Ken Latham considers decision making one of his critical functions. He says, "You can't give people a whole lot of information, pat them on the back, and say, 'The answer's there, go find it.' My job is to assimilate that information for them and give them my decision. You have to accept the responsibility and say, 'I've decided this is what you need.'"

Don't steer a customer all the way through the decision-making process and then turn the wheel over to him to negotiate the last mile of the unfamiliar road. If the customer knew what to do, he wouldn't need you. You are earning your money by being a decision maker. This includes making the final decision: what to invest in, how much to invest in it, and when to make the investment. If you expect a customer to make the final decision on his own, you'll be disappointed. You have to ask for the order.

Rarely will you make a recommendation when it will not be appropriate to take immediate action. The "when" to make an investment is "now." Nobody makes money just by watching investments. You will never buy at the exact low or sell at the exact high. Trying to time the financial markets perfectly will cost your customers money.

You will be wrong many, many times in your career, just as

the top money managers in the world have been. If you've truly put forth your best effort, you're going to be right more often than wrong. Don't finish a presentation with "Let's watch it for a while"; say, "Let's do it now!"

Successful brokers prospect themselves into situations where they can ask for the order. Once given the opportunity, they never hesitate. But there's one thing they do when they ask for the order that makes them even more successful.

SECRET OF SIX-FIGURE SUCCESS NUMBER FOUR: THINK BIG AND THEN EVEN BIGGER

When you ask for the order, think big. Don't let the amount of money in your wallet influence how much you think is in someone else's. There's a lot of money out there, more than you can imagine. If you ask for small orders, you'll never get anything but small orders. If you ask for big orders, you'll be amazed at how much more business you'll do.

Don't start your career by asking for small orders, thinking you'll work up to bigger ones. The principle is the same as for the people you prospect: call big people from day one, ask for big orders from day one. The best way to become a customer's "thousand share broker"—top financial advisor—is to act like a thousand share broker. When you start off by asking for small orders, it gives the distinct impression that you are a small-time broker, an impression that's difficult to overcome.

Don't be afraid of embarrassing a customer by asking for a big order. If they don't have the money, at least they'll be flattered. Keep in mind that most people will show you only the tip of the iceberg—only a small amount of their money—until they get to know you. Asking for a big order helps you get the full picture more quickly.

Bob Cranshaw adds this perspective: "I don't sell investments, I place them where they're needed. I'm careful not to put too many of a customer's eggs in one basket. But if you're going to invest in something, you have to invest enough to make it count."

Asking for a small order conveys the message to the customer that you really don't have much confidence in your recommendation—you're hedging. A few years ago, a young broker was prospecting a millionaire. The millionaire was favorably impressed by the broker and agreed to buy a stock if the broker could come up with a good idea. The broker came back to him with a great recommendation, and the prospect was thrilled. "How much should I buy?" he asked. The broker recommended one hundred shares. Abruptly the prospect soured on the whole idea. "If it's only worth one hundred shares, it can't be worth buying at all," he said.

If you want to do big business, ask for big orders. It doesn't take any more time to say "one thousand" instead of "one hundred."

DEVELOPING THE ACCOUNT: MAKING THE MOST OF WHAT YOU ALREADY HAVE

The number of new accounts you open is the number-one factor in your success. Right behind it is what you do with your accounts after you've opened them.

The amount of business you do each year is directly related to how many dollars your customers have invested with you. There is only so much commission a prudently invested dollar can generate each year. If you want to increase your business, you have to bring in new dollars.

New accounts are one source of new funds. Successful brokers make very good use of another source, however: their existing accounts. They know that the money the customer used to open the account is usually just a fraction of what is available. Successful brokers also know that just because an account was opened with one type of investment, this is not the only type of investment that's appropriate for the customer's needs. It's just the first piece in the puzzle.

TRUE PROFESSIONAL OR STOCK-OF-THE-DAY SALESMAN?
HOW TO TURN A CUSTOMER INTO A CLIENT

Right after you've opened a new account, you will find yourself at an important crossroad. At this point your customer is nothing more than a person who has done some business with you. You have two paths you can follow in your efforts to develop your relationship further. Only one will lead to a long-lasting relationship built on trust and respect. You want the customer to be more than someone who buys things from you. You want the customers to become clients: people who rely on your expertise and honesty in handling a very critical aspect of their lives.

Some brokers seem to envision all their customers dressed in Velcro. The brokers grab an investment, throw it at their customers, and hope that it sticks to a few. Eventually, customers catch on to a "stock-of-the-day" salesman. They realize that the never-ending "specials" are for one person's benefit only: the broker's. In the short run, a stock-of-the-day salesman can appear to be successful, but this is only an illusion. Underneath the big paychecks, you'll find an eroding customer base and constant headaches.

If you want your customers to become your clients, you have to stay on the path you started out on. You must be a professional problem solver. It doesn't matter how many answers you have, though, unless you have the questions to work on. This means that your customers must really open up to you. They will have to be comfortable with you both personally and professionally. That's not easy when you're dealing strictly over the phone. A rising star at Prudential-Bache Securities puts it this way: "I never try to open an account over the phone. I always go for the appointment. There's more lead time between my initial call and when I open the account, but when I open the account, it's with a substantial amount of money."

Once you've opened a new account, it's more imperative than ever that you meet with your customers and get to know them better, especially if you've never met before. Remember, this is a "people" business. You can accomplish far more, in terms of learning about the customer and building greater rapport, in a one-hour appointment than in weeks of phone conversation.

It's important that when you sit down with a customer for the first time you give him or her a complete financial check-up. The longer you wait to discuss their entire financial situation, the harder it will be to shake the narrow image of stockbrokers most people still have. You must impress upon customers how you view your job and tell them what you need to know so that you can be of the greatest service to them.

There's more to being a professional than knowledge and technique. "Do unto others as you would have them do unto you" should be at the core of every professional-client relationship. One young broker at Kidder, Peabody and Co. applies this philosophy to his business in this way: "I always try to picture myself as someone calling my parents. I wouldn't want anybody trying to sell them something they don't need." I believe that a similar thought is in the mind of every good broker.

THE CLIMB TO THE TOP

It is tempting to say that the formula for being a successful stock-broker can be reduced to three components: know what you're talking about, talk to a lot of people, and be a solver of financial problems. Mastering these skills will take you a long way toward your goal. Yet a baseball player doesn't make it to the Hall of Fame simply because he can hit, catch, and throw. He needs additional skills and qualities to reach the peak of his profession. The same is true for a stockbroker. If you want to achieve a six-figure income within three years, and go even higher in the years to come, you must go beyond the basics and emulate the superstars who have preceded you.

THE FAST START: REACHING THE FLASH POINTS

If you were to examine a chart showing the month-by-month earnings growth of a successful broker, you would see a nice, orderly uptrend, interrupted by some months where the earnings just seem to explode upward. Reaching those flash points, where your earnings are double or even triple those of your previous months, is vital to your success. It elevates your performance standards to a higher level, and once you know you can reach that level, you won't accept anything less from yourself.

Why do successful brokers hit flash points in their careers? Is it merely luck? Quite the contrary. Flash points are the result of extra effort and achievement over a period of time. The statement that "success breeds success" is not a cliché in this business; it's a basic principle. On the surface, opening a few extra accounts or doing an extra several thousand dollars in business each month may not seem crucial when you're starting out. After all, "there's always next month." If you are able to do it, however, you will be rewarded exponentially as time goes on. The little extras add up and feed your success more than is immediately apparent.

Extra accounts expand your sources of business. Extra prospecting calls get your name in front of more people. Extra orders increase your level of confidence. All these things act synergistically until suddenly your business starts to grow faster than seemed possible only weeks before. It isn't luck. You create your own opportunities through work and preparation.

Ken Latham recalls when his business hit a flash point for the first time. "All those seeds, all those calls suddenly hit. I was going along nicely, averaging about $10,000 a month in production. Then one day I did $9,000 in production—out of nowhere. People just called in and said, 'You know that $200,000 we've been talking about? Go ahead and put it into XYZ.' It really opened my eyes to how much I could really do."

Getting off to a fast start makes it possible to hit flash points more quickly and more often. On the other hand, the longer it takes you to get your business off the ground, the less it is likely that you will ever reach a point where your business increases suddenly and dramatically. A lack of success when starting out becomes increasingly difficult to overcome as the months pass.

Given the importance of getting off to a fast start, it's astounding how many new brokers approach their first few months haphazardly. They accept the results of their work as predetermined all too readily. If a new broker opens just four accounts in his first month, he may start to believe that he wasn't cut out to be a successful broker. This attitude can only lead to mediocrity. The difference between the superstars and the also-rans comes from expectations and effort.

SECRET OF SIX-FIGURE SUCCESS NUMBER FIVE: SET GOALS AND MAKE THE EFFORT TO ACHIEVE THEM

Few people have reached the tops of their professions by accident. To be successful, you must set performance goals right from the start and work to be sure you reach them. If you adopt an "I'll just wait and see what happens" approach toward your business, nothing much *will* happen.

Your goals should be high. You can't aim for acceptable performance and expect to achieve exceptional performance. Set yearly, monthly, weekly, and even daily goals for new accounts and production, and map out a strategy for achieving them. How many prospecting calls per day will it take to achieve your new account goal? How many nights will you work? How can you improve your product knowledge? How many appointments should you have a week? How many presentations will you have to make on your new investment idea? Major success comes at the end of a lengthy string of smaller achievements.

Richard Desiderio attributes much of his success to his ability to focus his efforts in the right direction. He says, "You've got to get your priorities straight, plan your work, and work your plan. Write down your goals and review your progress every day. Don't just look at them January first and then forget about them. Push yourself, but don't make your goals impossible. It's important to feel some success."

A lot of distance on the road to success is covered by going an extra mile each day, but extra effort can be wasted unless it's focused on a specific goal. When you can visualize the goals you're setting out to achieve, extra effort becomes effortless.

Too often effort is measured by hours. You may have spent twelve hours at the office, but did you do twelve hours of work, or even eight? There is no doubt that you will have to work long hours to be successful: a minimum of two nights a week plus Saturdays on top of ten-hour days. But logging in the hours doesn't necessarily mean that you will be successful. It's what you do with the time that makes the difference.

SECRET OF SIX-FIGURE SUCCESS NUMBER SIX: WORK HARD AND SMART

Putting your shoulder to the wheel doesn't mean that you can't use your brain. The wheel may be in motion, but are you moving ahead or are you spinning in a ditch? What you do each day is your responsibility; you're in business for yourself. Nobody will assign you work on a task-by-task basis until it's time to go home. If you go to work without a plan for the day and just "go with the flow," you'll discover that there is a long distance between you and success.

Bob Cranshaw believes that organization is more than a short-cut; it's a necessity. "My day planner is my most important tool outside of my phone and my quote machine. You have to know what you're going to be doing from the moment you walk into the office, right through the day. You can't just blunder into things and expect to get anything done."

Each day, before leaving your office, plan your work for the following day in detail. Make a list of the prospects and clients you will call and note what the objective of each call will be. Think about what operational problems need to be attended to, and what you are going to do to improve the quality of your product. There's a world of difference between "Tomorrow I think I'll make some prospecting calls" and "This is a list of the seventy prospects I will call before I leave the office tomorrow." Structure your work each day. Take control of your time. It's something to use, not just fill up.

You don't need to live at your office if you keep one simple rule in mind: when you're at the office, *work*! Brokerage offices are full of distractions. There's always someone willing to shoot the breeze; playing with your quote machine can be as addictive as the latest video game, and you don't even need quarters. Be keenly aware of the difference between being at the job and being on the job. Only the latter contributes to your success. It's not how long you make your workday, it's what you make of it that counts. The solid, well-planned ten-hour workday is a trademark of the successful broker.

THE SIX-MONTH SYNDROME

The advantages of getting your career into high gear quickly can be lost if you're not careful. Many brokers unwittingly derail their careers, some permanently, by succumbing to the Six-Month Syndrome.

After several months of tough prospecting, you will have a handful of clients. Clients are easier to call than prospects because they already know you. A call to a client is also more likely to put commission dollars in your pocket, and isn't that what the business is all about? Following the handful of investments you have on the books is fun. You never thought it was so easy to be a professional money manager. All of a sudden, however, you've done all the business you can possibly do with your handful of clients, and they're starting to wonder why you call them so often. Pretty soon your business is back to nothing, and there's no new business on the horizon. The euphoria of your fast start is replaced by panic. "What am I going to do now?" is a sign of the Six-Month Syndrome.

How can you avoid the Six-Month Syndrome? You avoid it by keeping in mind what made your first taste of success possible: prospecting.

SECRET OF SIX-FIGURE SUCCESS NUMBER SEVEN: NEVER STOP PROSPECTING

The more you prospect, the more your prospecting skills improve. Why stop using a hard-earned skill just when you've started to get really good at it? Successful brokers never stop prospecting.

Prospecting is like reading; you don't stop once you've learned how.

Ken Latham emphasizes the importance of prospecting for a broker on the way up. He remarks, "After two or three years, you're not a good prospector. You're the best there is. The experience factor makes you a tremendous prospector. This business is always changing, but some things will never change. You have to work hard, and you have to stay on the phone. The day you stop prospecting is the day you're going to be out of business, one year removed."

When you stop prospecting, your business stops growing. Your efforts to develop your existing accounts further are counteracted by clients moving out of town, passing away, losing interest, or simply running out of problems to solve. New blood is needed not only to expand your business, but to keep it stable. The bounties of a good market can delude you into thinking otherwise, but don't be fooled. The minute you stop prospecting you are stating loudly, "I am content to go no further and willing to risk going backward."

Once you attain a comfortable level of success, it's easy to fall into the trap of thinking, "Prospecting is for rookies. I'm above that now." Turn on your television; you'll see ads for IBM, General Motors, McDonald's, and General Electric, all leaders in their fields. You are never so big or so good that you don't need to advertise.

In a busy airport last year I ran into a broker friend whose annual production exceeds one million dollars a year. "How's business?" I asked. "Great! I'm going to open over fifty new accounts this month!" he imparted as he jogged off for his plane. He wasn't thinking dollars, although that would be easy with a $400,000-plus annual income. He wasn't resting on his past accomplishments, either. He knows that prospecting—bringing in new accounts—is the most important part of the success equation.

How can a broker generate over a million dollars in production and still find the time to open two hundred or three hundred new accounts in a year? You can use a technique you used your first day in the business: let your clients help you prospect.

SECRET OF SIX-FIGURE SUCCESS NUMBER EIGHT: ASK FOR REFERRALS

Information about your clients and their investments is strictly confidential. There's no reason, though, that your clients have to keep the good job you're doing for them a secret.

From time to time a client will refer a friend or business associate your way, but why sit back and wait? Most of your clients aren't aware that you are always seeking to expand your business and that you welcome new accounts. Many don't routinely discuss their investments with their friends and associates; they don't get a chance to talk about you. You'll find that your clients will be happy to recommend your services to others, but only if you ask them to.

One simple question—"By the way, Mr. Client, who else do you know who might benefit from my services?"—can increase your business by 50 percent or more. The secret is to get into the habit of asking it.

How powerful can referrals be in building your business? Valerie Freeman says, "If I tried to put a price on the value of referrals to my business, no matter how high I went it would still be too low. I opened nineteen accounts last month. Eighteen were from referrals."

Every time you speak with a client you should be asking yourself, "Is this an appropriate time to ask for a referral?" Particularly good times to ask for referrals are when a new client is opening an account or when an existing client is making an investment. The clients are bound to be feeling good about you then. There will also be times when it will seem inappropriate to ask for a referral. This is okay, but make sure you've made a conscious decision not to ask, not simply forgotten.

When should you start asking for referrals? The minute you open your first account, if not sooner. Soon you'll be opening accounts on referrals from clients who were referrals themselves. Think of the multiplier effect this can have on the growth of your business. Ask everyone, not just your best clients. One of Valerie Freeman's referrals turned out to be a multimillion-dollar account. The referral was from a client with $2,000 invested in the stock market. You never know who knows whom.

What about asking prospects for referrals? It's likely that you'll want to hold off from asking a good prospect for referrals until you've opened the account. However, if you have determined that you will not have any further contact with a prospect, even if it's during the first and only call, you have nothing to lose by asking for a referral. You'll be surprised how many times you'll be rewarded for the little extra effort this takes.

WHAT INVESTORS REALLY WANT FROM THEIR BROKER

If you asked a group of investors what they want most from a broker, what do you think would be the most common response? You probably think it would be "He makes money for me!" But survey after survey conducted by the brokerage industry shows that other qualities are ranked higher. Knowing what these are will help you be more successful. After all, the easiest way to keep customers satisfied is to give them what they want.

The two qualities of a broker rated most important by investors are:

Honesty and Integrity. Behind every dollar you invest, there is a person. Each dollar represents his hard work, his dreams, and his trust in you. Your clients expect to be treated with the respect they deserve. Your integrity must be irreproachable, and your honesty unyielding. Anything less on your part is unacceptable. In this department, 99 percent is no better than zero percent.

Service. The quality of the service that backs a product up can be as important as the quality of the product itself. No matter how terrific your new car is, if the dealer keeps dragging his feet on fixing a faulty windshield wiper you may never go back to him again.

Compared to making a thousand-share stock investment, chasing down an errant dividend check, confirming a purchase price, or mailing some requested information can seem unimportant; so unimportant, in fact, that you might keep putting such things off until you forget about them. Your client doesn't share your forgetfulness. Chances are that the longer it takes you to attend to her requests, the greater her level of irritation. You'll be giving the impression that all you care about is commissions. (Isn't that what you thought about your balky car dealer?)

Good service isn't a frill demanded by unreasonable customers; it's a vital component of any quality product. Richard Desiderio believes that "You're only as good as your service. Everybody's got something to sell. It's what you add to what you're selling that makes you special. You have to take care of your customers."

Minor details become nagging details only if you let them. Remember, if it's important to the customer, it's important to you. Adopt a "same day" policy. Make sure that you (or your secretary) take care of all customer requests and administrative details on the same day problems occur. It's simply not worth losing a client over a detail that turns into a debacle.

Don't confuse good service with slavery, however. There are investors who make tremendous demands on their brokers' time. You cannot do a good job for your other clients and expand your business if your time is being taken up by giving quotes and hour-by-hour market analyses to a few. If one of these "time vampires" latches on to you, politely inform him that you are unable to provide him with the type of service he requires and refer him to your manager.

When you are starting out, do resist the temptation to over-service your customers. When your business expands, you will be unable to keep up your frequent and lengthy chats on the state of the world and everything in it. In addition, when you act as though you have plenty of time on your hands, people start to wonder why.

Tell your clients right at the beginning that you will call them only when you feel it is warranted. Don't become a stranger, though—stay in touch. Send your clients information that is pertinent to their investments. Let them know you are thinking about them. If a month or two goes by and you haven't had a reason to talk to a client, give him a call anyway. A five-minute update on his investments is the best way to prevent the "my broker never calls me" syndrome.

WHAT INVESTORS LIKE LEAST ABOUT THEIR BROKERS

Every broker gives investors advice on when to buy, but many brokers ignore the second half of the transaction—when to sell. Don't assume that once you've directed a client into an investment, he can find his way out on his own.

The biggest complaint raised by investors about their brokers is "My broker never tells me when to sell!" This really means, "My broker never tells me what to do with losing investments." Calling a client who has made a profit is easy. (Sometimes it's so easy that an investment is sold before it even comes close to fulfilling its potential.) When an investment goes down, though, it's easy to imagine the investor becoming a vicious Doberman attacking you through the phone. In reality the investor is just waiting for your professional advice. The longer he has to wait, the greater the chances that he won't be your client much longer.

SECRET OF SIX-FIGURE SUCCESS NUMBER NINE: AVOID BIG LOSSES

Successful brokers stick mostly to conservative investments. Even a conservative approach doesn't guarantee a stable of solid winners, though. Even the best investment minds end up with some losers amidst the thoroughbreds. It's what you do with the losers that's important.

Keeping your investment losses to a minimum will keep you on the track to success. The old Wall Street adage, "Cut your losses short and let your profits run," is good advice. There are two reasons for this.

1. The larger your losses, the greater your successes have to be to attain even a moderate return on a client's portfolio. If you lose 50 percent on an investment, your next investment has to double just to get back to even. One big loser can negate the perfectly acceptable performance of the rest of your investment selections.

2. The greater the loss, the more intense the client's dissatisfaction. Putting it simply, people don't like to lose money, and the more they lose, the more they dislike the loss and anything connected with it. By avoiding large losses, you'll not only keep the client happy, you'll keep the client.

Bob Cranshaw doesn't ignore an investment when it goes down. He says, "I'm very disciplined about limiting my losses—I want my clients' money to grow. It only makes sense to let the flowers bloom and pull the weeds as soon as they come up."

Successful brokers don't see taking a loss as an admission of incompetence. They see it as their professional responsibility. The fact that you will have losing investments is a given. Nobody says that you have to stand helplessly by and watch an investment go down while hoping that it will turn around tomorrow. More often than not it won't turn around and go right back up, it will sink and stay put for quite some time.

A simple statement at the end of a sale will make picking up the phone to recommend taking a loss easier: "Mr. Client, I will monitor this investment and will let you know immediately of any important developments." Tell your clients that you will not stick with losing investments beyond a certain point and that you will recommend appropriate action if that point is reached. Don't become a member of the "tomorrow it might go back up" prayer society. It is your job to protect and preserve the client's capital. Picking up the phone will accomplish that far better than wishful thinking. Don't let a psychological barrier stand between you and your serving your client.

SECRET OF SIX-FIGURE SUCCESS NUMBER TEN: ACCEPT AND WELCOME CHANGE

The terrain on your journey to success will be constantly changing and so will the vehicles that will take you there. An oasis of opportunity will become a mirage. Your transportation may become outdated. How you deal with changes can shorten or prolong your trip.

Changes in the financial markets create new investment opportunities. New investments or an expansion of services offered by your firm can help you meet your clients' needs better. New technology can make it easier to provide your clients with more and better service.

Successful brokers know that the world is constantly changing. They stay in step with the changes. It is impossible to compete in today's environment with yesterday's products.

9

DO YOU HAVE WHAT IT TAKES?

The decision to become a stockbroker should not be made casually. The money and prestige may appeal to you, but you shouldn't let them blind you. The important question isn't whether you would *like* to be a successful stockbroker, it's whether you *could* be a successful stockbroker. Many individuals who are intelligent and personable have found that these qualities alone aren't enough. Successful brokers have a certain personal chemistry that propels them to the top.

This chapter describes the qualities you need to become a successful broker. Read it carefully. Successful stockbrokers will tell you that theirs is the best job in the world; others who have tried and come up short of the mark will tell you that their time as a broker was one of the most unsettling experiences of their lives.

DOES THE WORLD OF INVESTING APPEAL TO YOU?

Don't let a lack of familiarity with investments prohibit you from considering becoming a stockbroker. The majority of stockbrokers had little or no background in investments before entering the field. Knowledge can be acquired. What separates successful brokers from unsuccessful ones is the enthusiasm with which they pursue knowledge of the field. Investing turns them on. Successful brokers enjoy the challenge of investing and thrive on the dynamics and nuances of the financial world. Their enthusiasm for their craft ignites their entire business.

Being a zealous student of investing won't guarantee your success. The industry has a significant population of also-rans who were experts. It can be a prominent factor in your success when combined with the right attitude and hard work, however.

Does the world of investing appeal to you? There are a number of ways to find out before making a career change. These include the following.

1. College and adult education courses. Many colleges offer courses in investing on a noncredit basis, usually at times convenient for working adults. The give-and-take atmosphere of the classroom will help you overcome any initial anxiety you may have about the subject matter. An added advantage is that the courses are often taught by a local stockbroker, who can give you a feeling for the business.
2. Investment clubs. An investment club is a group of people who collectively invest regular, usually modest, contributions by the members. Belonging to an investment club can be fun, educational, and even profitable. Since all investment decisions are made by the entire group, belonging to an investment club can be an excellent introduction to the psychology of investing and the many ways in which people approach it.
3. The media. There are a number of books, newspapers, magazines, and television shows that cover investing in an accessible manner (see the Appendix). Don't expect to make sense of the material immediately, but after a

> while your interest in investing will either be piqued or
> will fizzle out.
>
> 4. Investing. The best way to find out if you like the water
> is to jump in and splash around a little. Set aside a sum
> of money you can afford to invest and identify a financial
> need you would like to address. Then try to find the best
> way to meet your need and put your solution into action.
> The entire process of selecting and tracking your in-
> vestment will give you good insight into a key aspect of
> being a stockbroker.

DO YOU HAVE WHAT IT TAKES?

Successful brokers come in all shapes and sizes. Their backgrounds are a perfect example of diversity. They do have some
things in common, however: the personal traits that make them
successful. On the surface this may seem obvious, but each trait
is a critical factor in success. The traits are discussed here.

Concern. Stockbrokers are in the "people business." How much
do people matter to you? You must genuinely care about helping
other people. You are literally dealing with people's lives. If you
have any doubt that this requires compassion and honesty, this
isn't the career for you.

Motivation. To travel the road to success, you will need strong
internal drive. Everyone wants to be on top, but not everyone
can harness the desire and turn it into action. Without motivation, dreams remain dreams.

Motivation is a combination of desire, pride, and ego. The
greater your desire to succeed at something, the greater your
effort. The more pride you take in your work, the better it will
be. A strong ego won't let you rest until you've achieved your
goals.

Are you a dreamer or a doer? Do you try to be the best when
you take on a new job or activity, or are you content to stay with
the pack? Do you take pride in everything you do? To succeed
as a broker, you have to want to help other people, but you also
have to want to help yourself.

Ability to Communicate. The best ideas in the world are useless unless they reach an audience. The size and receptivity of your audience, and therefore your level of success, depend greatly on your communication skills. Your verbal skills, your ability to listen, your appearance, and your personality are all important components of your communications arsenal. Hardly a minute will go by when you won't be using at least one of them.

Not only must you be a good communicator, but you must have the self-confidence to put your skills to use. Can you express yourself even when you have to think on your feet? Do you listen to what other people have to say, or do you close your ears when you close your mouth? Are you concerned with looking your best, not only in your own eyes but in the eyes of others? Do you work well with other people? You don't have to be the most popular person in town, but people do have to like you and feel comfortable with you.

Discipline. Motivation is raw energy. It needs to be properly directed to be effective. That direction comes from discipline. Without discipline, goals become compromised, details get overlooked, deadlines are extended, and difficult work gets ignored. You cannot be successful unless you have the discipline to do everything necessary, not just whatever is easy or convenient.

Are you a "do-it-now" person or do you habitually leave things until the last minute? Can you develop a plan of action and stick to it or do you depend more on improvisation and chance to direct your life? Do you quit work when the job is finished or when the whistle blows? Do you have a positive mental attitude or are you always looking for reasons for not doing something? The obstacles you will encounter can be overcome only if you have discipline.

Evaluate yourself carefully in the four areas of concern, motivation, ability to communicate, and discipline. If you don't quite measure up, don't throw in the towel. Having three out of the four traits allows hope for improvement. A four-cylinder engine can run on three cylinders; the ride just won't be as smooth. Also, although it's impossible to learn how to be concerned for others, it is possible to learn how to improve your communication skills and work habits. As for motivation, often all a plant needs to flourish is the right soil.

THE DEMANDS OF THE JOB

There's also more to being a successful broker than meeting the challenges of the profession. A broker must cope successfully with the demands of the job that come to meet him. These demands fall into three categories: emotional demands, demands on time, and physical demands.

Emotional. Successful brokers are good decision makers; they don't avoid having to make choices. A broker must be able to make decisions that involve thousands or even hundreds of thousands of dollars, sometimes in a matter of seconds. Even conservative investing is far from risk free, so a broker must be willing to accept risk.

The markets will test a broker's judgment over and over. A bad investment may put him or her in the depths of despair, but brokers still owe their clients sound, rational advice. If they can't put their emotions aside, they'll avoid making decisions altogether and become "sideline brokers." Confusing their own inability to take risks with serving the client's best interests, these brokers help neither their clients nor themselves.

Entrepreneurs are risk takers by definition. If a broker's emotions can't handle the uncharted waters of risk, he or she is better off remaining on shore.

Time. Becoming a successful stockbroker requires a tremendous commitment of time. The sixty hours a broker needs to spend each week building his (or her) business limits activities outside the office. A late dinner at home and an hour or two of reading may be all he has time for on a weekday. As a rule, Saturday mornings are spent at the office, not at the golf course or the beach. A broker may also spend part of Sunday doing research, updating his investment plan, and planning the week ahead. Obviously, sacrifices have to be made.

Even if a broker can devote the necessary time, maintaining the commitment is difficult without the support of those close to him or her. The time demands made upon a broker in the first several years may mean that a tennis game gets cancelled, the lawn grows a little high, dinners are less-than-four-star and that Friday night means falling asleep on the couch right after "Wall Street Week." A broker's spouse and children have to help carry the ball; they must understand that everyone stands to benefit if the broker's goals are reached.

Time is an important ingredient in productivity. A broker has to be able to contribute enough of it.

Physical. A broker doesn't get paid for simply being in her office. She has to make things happen. That means always being "up." People respond positively to individuals who exude a positive dynamism. Nobody wants to do business with a broker who sounds uninterested, half-asleep, or under stress. Long sedentary hours in the office, on-the-go eating habits, the constant mental stress can put a drag on a broker's system and make the extra distance hard going. A broker has to have the strength it takes to put in a long and productive day.

IS THIS REALLY THE CAREER FOR YOU?

If you're thinking "so far, so good," do you start sending out resumes and making phone calls? Not yet. There's still more for you to consider.

Being a stockbroker isn't a job; it's a personal business venture. As in any business, there is a failure rate. Between 40 and 50 percent of all new stockbrokers are out of the business before the end of their second years.

What are the causes of this high turnover? A minor percentage of failures can be attributed to "hiring mistakes"—people who shouldn't have been hired in the first place—but this occurs in every industry. Why do some people, who are as bright, personable, and motivated as the brokers who stay in the business, experience failure, often for the first time in their lives? It comes down to the reason that most businesses fail: lack of customers.

Stockbrokers who fail to stay in business usually are unable to perform the first or the last step in the prospecting process effectively.

The first step in prospecting is picking up the phone. For some people, the thought of contacting a total stranger brings on a gut-wrenching, nerve-racking feeling that's similar to the one you experienced the first time you asked someone out on a date. It's impossible to make scores of prospecting calls each day when every dial of the phone is a traumatic experience.

"Phone fear" can sometimes be overcome by determination and hard work. However, I believe that in many people it is a deep-rooted phobia. If you have any question about your ability to prospect, volunteer to "cold call" for a charity fund-raising drive. Once you get going, you should start to relax and enjoy yourself. If the hours fly by instead of dragging, chances are good that you'll be able to pick up the phone and prospect if you really want to. Be totally honest with yourself, though; if your phone seems to weigh a ton, you won't succeed.

The last step in prospecting is recommending an appropriate action to the prospect and asking for the order. Even after walking the prospect down the aisle, you still have to say "Let's do it!" Some brokers find these words impossible to say and substitute "What do you think?" or "Let's watch it for a while." These substitutes just simply don't work. No matter how good your prospecting skills are, you cannot open enough accounts to be successful if you are a perpetual vacillator. If the thought of telling other people what to do with their money seems like a burden instead of a challenge to you, you'll have trouble turning prospects into customers.

Several years ago, one of my better clients invited me to dinner. His interest in investing had sparked a desire in him to become a stockbroker. Over the course of the evening I described the ins and outs of the profession, spending most of the time describing prospecting. My client decided to pursue his ambition. Despite a lack of any type of business background (he was an artist), his knowledge and winning personality landed him a position at a well-respected firm. We kept in touch. From our conversations it was obvious that he knew what he had to do to be successful, but after a year and a half he left the field. Why? "I never could really handle the prospecting," he told me.

These words are repeated over and over by those who join the ranks of former brokers every year.

THE FINAL DECISION

The time you've spent reading this chapter isn't enough for you to have reached a decision. It will require serious thinking. Only if you're right for the job will the job be right for you. You will want to discuss the matter with your family. If you have a broker, get his or her thoughts about the business. A view from the front line will be valuable.

If after careful consideration you're ready to go, it's time for you to make your first sale—of yourself.

10

HOW TO GET THE JOB

Now that you've decided you want to be a stockbroker, it's time to go out and find a job. There are a few things you need to consider first, however.

WHERE YOU START IS WHERE YOU STAY

Before taking the first step in your job search, you need to think about where you live and where you'd like to live. If these are two different places, now's the time to resolve the conflict.

There are many great things about being a stockbroker, but geographic mobility isn't one of them. As in any other business that is based on serving people in a local area, you can't pick your business up and take it with you. Every day you are putting down deeper and deeper roots. Experience can be transplanted, but the fruits of your labors can't. Most investors would rather deal with someone locally, because it's difficult to get personalized service at a distance. No matter how much they like you, the vast majority of your clients will stay put if you move out of town. Also, not only is it difficult to walk away from a growing business and all the time and effort it represents, it's even more difficult to get cranked up to do it all over again somewhere else.

You should be absolutely sure that you want to stay in the area you'll be working in. You should also consider the effect your immobility will have on your spouse's career.

I've had many a new broker come to me and say, "I'm not sure I want to stay in Biscuit City. What should I do?" The best scenario is no longer possible for them, but it is still possible for you. Think about it beforehand. If you want to move to another area, now's the time.

WHO ARE YOUR JOB PROSPECTS?

Looking for a brokerage firm to work for is like putting together a list of prospects. Start at the top, with the firms in your area that are the most desirable to work for. You can have only one job, so aim for the best.

Begin your search by opening the Yellow Pages in the phone directory for your area. Under the heading "Investment Securities" or "Stock and Bond Brokers" you will find a listing of every brokerage firm. To qualify for your initial list a firm must be:

1. A New York Stock Exchange member. Not all member firms will specify "NYSE member" in their listings. If there's any question, a quick phone call will provide the answer.
2. A full-service firm. The firm must emphasize a full range of investments and services. Discount brokers do not have the earnings potential enjoyed by full-service brokers. Be aware that there are firms that profess to be full-service but in fact emphasize one particular investment area, such as tax shelters, mutual funds, or over-the-counter "penny" stocks.

Looking at your list you'll see names that range from the well-known to the unfamiliar. You can't rank the names on your list by impressions; anybody can advertise. You need the real story behind the name.

BIG VERSUS SMALL: WHO'S BETTER?

Brokerage firms can be divided into three size categories: national firms (firms with offices coast to coast), regional firms (firms covering a region of the country), and local firms (firms with offices only in one city or a small area).

One of the longest running debates in the brokerage industry centers on the comparative advantages of working for a major firm versus those of a regional or local firm. Asking a manager from each side to extol the virtues of working for his firm might yield the following responses.

Major firm manager: "My firm can offer a broker better resources, a better reputation, and greater attention to the broker's needs."

Small firm manager: "My firm can offer a broker better resources, a better reputation, and greater attention to the broker's needs."

Who's right? So much depends on the individual office that it's impossible to make a blanket statement about the relative merits of various brokerage firms. In fact, it's quite possible to have two offices of the same firm located just blocks apart, and have the brokers in one office be far more productive and happy than their neighbors.

There are several potential advantages to working for a major firm. A handful of firms have become household names through their sheer size and advertising. The recognition factor can be helpful when you are prospecting if it's backed by a good reputation. Major firms also generally lead the way in the development of new products and services. If a new idea catches on with the public, this can be a tremendous competitive advantage. Merrill Lynch's Cash Management Account—a pioneering brokerage account with banklike features introduced in 1977—gave their brokers a lead on the competition in that segment of the market that has never been relinquished.

A smaller firm often offers the prospect of a more personal

environment. The smaller number of brokers makes it easier to communicate with people throughout the firm, from the president to the operations clerks.

The thing to remember is that you're not going to be working with the entire country, only with the people in your area. The most important of those people are the people in your office. They determine the outcome of the "who's better?" debate.

INSIDE FOUR WALLS

It's not surprising that the "people business" concept is just as important within your office as it is in your dealings with the public. After all, a brokerage office is nothing more than four walls and a roof containing an assortment of office equipment. It's the people who work in the office that provide its character.

No person plays a more vital role in an office than the manager. The manager does the hiring—he decides who's on the team. It's up to him to manage his team collectively and individually in a way that's to the best advantage of everyone, including the customers. In many respects the branch office system of a brokerage firm is a lot like the feudal system in medieval times. Each manager is lord of the manor, and how much you like the country depends in large part on whose territory you live in.

Here are a few of the important questions that management provides the answers to.

- Does the firm enjoy a good reputation locally?
- Does the office have a good working environment?
- How much personal attention will you receive?
- Is the office run efficiently?
- Are the resources offered by the firm used to full advantage?

It's no wonder that brokers who switch firms list "management" frequently as the reason. It's important to be with the right people.

The best way to find the right people is to ask around. Talk to your friends, neighbors, parents—anyone who has a local brokerage account. Find out their opinions on their firm and their broker. If someone has good things to say, ask for a referral; that is, ask if you can use their name to introduce yourself to their broker.

Most brokers are willing to spend a few minutes with someone interested in their profession. You'll be very likely to get a candid view both of the profession and the office a broker works in, the pluses and the minuses. Brokers are used to giving frank advice— all you have to do is ask. A potential bonus is that if you make a favorable impression, the broker might report your interest to the manager, helping to open the door for you.

If at all possible, try to visit an office during business hours. You'll be able to get a sense of the dynamics of the office. Is there a lot of activity, or is everyone sitting around waiting for the phones to ring?

Spend the same amount of effort and care in looking for the right firm as you would in looking for a new house. You'll be spending almost as much time in your office as you will at home.

GETTING AN INTERVIEW—HOW TO AVOID BEING JUST ANOTHER APPLICANT ON FILE

Once you've determined your top choices of a firm, it's time to make some calls. An understanding of brokerage office hiring practices will help you with the right approach.

Brokerage offices generally don't advertise when there's an opening. Positions are usually filled quietly, one or two at a time, from an existing pool of applicants. More often than not, an inquiry about a job will elicit a "not currently hiring but you're welcome to fill out an application" response. You can't file an application and then just sit back and wait for a call, however. You have to work your way to the front of the line.

In reality, an office manager is always hiring. There's always a space for the right candidate. No manager is going to turn away someone who has star potential. You should have the same attitude in applying as you would have in prospecting a wealthy investor who already has several brokers. If you're really good, there's plenty of room for you.

As in prospecting, the most effective way to sell yourself is face to face. This means an interview with the manager. The only

way you can count on getting one is to take the offensive. Here
are the three steps that should get you in the door.

1. Send your resume with a cover letter. Your resume should
   state your occupational objective specifically. Being a
   broker is not a job for people who are just looking for a
   job. Emphasize in your letter that this is really what you
   want to do. Highlight anything you've done that demonstrates an ability to stick to things and run the extra
   mile. What you've done isn't as important as how well
   you've done it. Don't exaggerate, though. If you're hired,
   your background will be thoroughly checked. Direct your
   cover letter to the manager by name. State that you will
   be calling at a designated time (allow about a week) to
   arrange an interview.
2. Call to set up an interview. Attitude is everything. Think
   "when," not "if." You are calling to arrange your interview, not to see if you could possibly get one.
3. Don't take no for an answer. Be businesslike, but be
   firm and persistent. If the manager's secretary says "no,"
   politely insist on talking to the manager. Recruiting good
   brokers is an important part of the manager's job. Even
   if your resume doesn't stand out, your determination
   will.

PREPARING FOR THE INTERVIEW

An interview is like any other sales presentation. You can't walk
in unprepared and expect to walk out with an order. You can't
read someone else's script and expect to sound convincing. Your
answers to questions have to come from you. This requires thought
and preparation on your part.

During your interview, the manager is likely to concentrate on
the following three topics.

1. Why do you want to be a broker? Why do you want to
   work for this firm? What is it that appeals to you about
   the job? Remember, there's more to the job of broker
   than investing. The manager wants to find out if you
   know what the job is really all about. Be sure to let him

know why you selected his firm. You want to avoid the impression that you're knocking on doors randomly.

2. What would you do if you were a broker? The manager will be judging your commitment. Are you willing to do whatever it takes to be successful? This means not only putting in the necessary time but also doing other necessary things. Nothing is more important in the manager's eyes than your ability and willingness to prospect. Show that you have concrete ideas on how you'd build your business.

3. What have you done that demonstrates that you can do the job? The manager will be looking for evidence that you are the right person for the job. Do you have a track record of success and the drive to take on challenges— even run through a brick wall to meet them? Anything you've done that shows you're an overachiever should be mentioned, whether at work, at school, in athletics, or in the community.

Incidentally, there's no such thing as dressing too conservatively for your interview. The conservative dress code of Wall Street extends throughout the industry. Even if business dress in your area is on the casual side, there's a very good chance that the office manager is from another part of the country. Play it safe.

HOW TO TURN A "NO" INTO A "YES"

If your interview ends with, "When can you start?" congratulations! But if it doesn't, do you take no for an answer and tell yourself, "Well, at least I tried"? A successful broker never let a little rejection stand in the way.

A Bear, Stearns and Co. manager puts it this way. "The candidate who really wants to be a broker won't turn away if he gets turned down." In other words, don't be afraid to be assertive. Ask for another interview. Be polite, but let the manager know that you think you're right for the job and would like another opportunity to prove it.

I know many brokers who got their jobs because they didn't accept the first "no" as a final answer. Virtually every manager in the business started as a broker and can empathize with stick-to-itiveness. Recently a manager told me about a broker in his office, "I hired him only because I ran out of the energy to keep turning him down. Now he's a million-dollar producer."

A WORD ABOUT STARTING SALARY

Because the financial opportunities for brokers are so tremendous, the starting salaries aren't. While you're training, you'll be paid a modest salary, typically between $900 and $1,200 a month, although major firms will sometimes pay more to a person with an established track record in business who's changing careers. The point is this. If you can pay your bills, be content. You can't expect someone to set you up in business and pay you a big salary as well. You're going to have to make some sacrifices. Just keep your eye on the payoff.

WHAT TO LOOK FORWARD TO IF YOU SUCCEED

Once you've become registered, your firm may continue to pay you a salary for a limited time while you build your business. This can be a big help in your first few months. You'll have enough on your mind without having to count pennies. But if you're successful, your base salary, whatever it is, will soon become irrelevant.

Here is a guide for your first three years.

YEAR	PRODUCTION TOTAL*	INCOME
1	$80,000	$30,000
2	$160,000	$60,000
3	$270,000	$100,000

Good luck!

*Note: Production totals, the amount of commissions generated by a broker, are approximate. The exact total necessary to achieve the stated income levels will vary from firm to firm.

EPILOGUE

LOOKING INTO THE FUTURE

Few industries have undergone a more sweeping transformation in recent years than the brokerage industry. Indeed, if a Rip van Brokerwinkle were to awake today from a lengthy slumber, he would find few familiar things amidst the intensified competition, the technological advancements, and the many new products and services at his disposal. Behind the headlines dominated by the spectacular performance of the financial markets, Rip would find brokerage firms pushing as hard as ever in their efforts to gain an advantage over their competitors.

In recent years the race to capture investors has centered on quantity; that is, who can build the most complete financial supermarket. Although this race is likely to continue as long as there are willing participants, a new race possibly with far greater impact is just beginning. The focus of this race is on quality— who can do the best job for the client. There may be a lot of products available, but an investment only becomes a good investment if it's purchased at the right time by the right person.

Investors are more knowledgeable today than ever before. The number who confuse ad campaigns, sales tactics, and marketing gimmicks with quality personalized investment decisions grows smaller every day. There's no substitute for protecting the client's money and helping it grow, something that successful brokers have known right along.

The winners of the quality race will be the brokerage firms who stress the fundamentals of the business over bells and whistles. Brokers dedicated to truly serving their clients are likely to find their firms to be very supportive of their efforts.

There are industry watchers, however, who believe that brokers will eventually take a back seat to, or even be replaced by, technological advances and direct marketing. Are stockbrokers costly middlemen facing extinction? The answer is no.

There is no computer, satellite, mail-in form, or hot-line that can take the place of a broker in analyzing a client's true needs and objectives, selecting the right investment(s), and providing the motivation to take action. The broker who views technology not as an enemy but as an aid can only improve the quality of the service provided to clients. A stockbroker provides a client with a single, centralized point of accountability and direction for his or her account, a feature that cannot be provided by a staff of specialists.

Although there will always be a percentage of investors willing and able to steer their own ships, the majority will continue to prefer, if not require, working one-on-one with a skilled professional. The financial seas through which brokers will pilot their clients in the years ahead promise to be as stormy as ever. How far will the bull market in stocks run? How low will interest rates fall? What will the ramifications of changes in the tax code be? When will inflation make a comeback? (It's difficult to think about this now, but one way or another, it's going to happen.) What investments will be most attractive? The answers to these questions will provide tremendous opportunities for stockbrokers and investors alike. May you profit from the opportunities, regardless of on which side of a broker's desk you're seated.

APPENDIX
RECOMMENDED READING

Getting Started

How to Buy Stocks, by Louis Engel and Brendan Boyd (Bantam). The best starting point for a novice, but even the most experienced investor will find this classic to be informative. Excellent graphics and illustrations make **Understanding Wall Street**, by Jeffrey B. Little and Lucien Rhodes (Liberty), an excellent companion volume.

Words of Wall Street: 2000 Investment Terms Defined, by Allan Pessin and Joseph Ross (Dow Jones-Irwin). This reference guide to Wall Street lingo takes the guesswork out of financial reading.

Extraordinary Popular Delusions and the Madness of Crowds, by Charles Mackay (Harmony). Written in 1841, this study of investment crazes, mass mania, and scams is just as relevant today as on the day it was first published. You could easily substitute gold or oil at the turn of the 1980s for tulip bulbs in the 1630s.

More Advanced

The Money Masters, by John Train (Penguin). A study of the philosophies and techniques of nine of the all-time best money managers.

The Intelligent Investor, by Benjamin Graham (Harper and Row). The most respected investment analyst of the past fifty years, Graham's value-oriented approach to investing that will help investors for generations to come.

The New Contrarian Investment Strategy, by David Dreman (Random House). Investing according to the new Golden Rule: "Do unlike others."

On the Newsstand

Money. Covers a wide range of personal finance topics in an informative and easy-to-read style.

Forbes. As insightful as it is entertaining. (Other listings on a broker's reading list are *Fortune, Barron's* and *Business Week.*)

The Wall Street Journal. The most widely read financial information source. If you think it's just about dollars and cents, you're in for a pleasant surprise.

Other Sources

"Wall $treet Week." Louis Rukeyser's television show has convinced millions that investing is a far from boring or abstract subject. The special guests are of the highest caliber.

Dick Davis Digest (P.O. Box 2828, Ocean View Station, Miami Beach, Florida 33140). Highlights and investment ideas drawn from a wide range of investment newsletters, all tied together by the editor's knowledgeable commentary.

American Association of Individual Investors (612 N. Michigan Ave., Chicago, Illinois 60611). A nonprofit group offering a range of educational programs and materials tailored to the individual investor.

National Association of Investor Corporations (1515 E. 11th Mile Road, Royal Oak, Michigan 48067). Formerly the National Association of Investor Clubs. Membership is now open to individuals.

INDEX

123

ABOUT THE AUTHOR

Bruce Eaton is a leading authority on financial service training. His combined experience as a stockbroker, marketing manager, and Assistant Vice President–Senior Training Consultant with Merrill Lynch has provided him with a rare insight into the marketing of financial products and services. Now heading his own training organization, he resides in Plainsboro, New Jersey, with his wife, Linda.